P9-CST-545

The Invention of Culture

Roy Wagner

The Invention of Culture

Revised and Expanded Edition

The University of Chicago Press
Chicago and London

The University of Chicago Press, Chicago 60637
The University of Chicago Press, Ltd., London

©1975, 1981 by Roy Wagner
All rights reserved. Published 1975
Revised and expanded edition 1981
Printed in the United States of America

85   2 3 4 5

Library of Congress Cataloging in Publication Data

Wagner, Roy.
    The invention of culture.

    Includes bibliographical references and index.
    1. Culture. 2. Anthropology. 2. Symbolism. I. Title.
GN357.W33   1981   306   80-25482
ISBN 0-226-86933-4
ISBN 0-226-86934-2 (pbk.)

To David M. Schneider

Contents

Preface

The idea that man invents his own realities is not a new one; it is found in such diverse philosophies as the Muta'zilla of Islam and the teachings of Buddhism, as well as in many much less formal systems of thought. Perhaps it has always been known to man. Nevertheless, the prospect of introducing this idea to an anthropology and a culture that wants very much to control its own realities (as all cultures do) is a difficult one. An undertaking such as this one therefore requires far more encouragement than the more staid projects of ethnography, and I can safely say that without the strong and interested encouragement of David M. Schneider this book would not have been written. Its theoretical inspiration, moreover, owes much to his work, much that is too germinal to be easily acknowledged, as well as his very explicit insights into modern American culture, which are basic to what has become a consuming interest of my discourse.

Friends at Northwestern University and the University of Western Ontario have added the considerable support of their ideas and interest. In particular, I would like to acknowledge my gratitude to the members of my E70 seminar in the spring of 1972, Helen Beale, Barbara Jones, Marcene Marcoux, and Robert Welsch, and to John Schwartzman, Alan Darrah, and John Farella for the benefit of their counsel and conversation. John Gehman, Stephen Tobias, Lee Guemple, and Sandie Shamis provided a lively counterpoint of ideation during a strategically formative stage in the writing. A part of Chapter 2 was read in April 1972, at a Monday afternoon seminar of the Department of Anthropology at the University of Chicago, and received the benefit of the inspired criticism and commentary that are so much a part of those occasions. A version of Chapter 3 was read at Northern Illinois University in April 1973, and I would like to thank particularly M. Jamil Hanifi and Cecil H. Brown for their helpful comments and insights expressed there. Terse but invaluable commentary and criticism was proferred by my colleague Johannes Fabian while casting (unsuccessfully) for fish at Sturgeon Bay, Wisconsin, in June 1972. My wife, Sue, displayed considerable forbearance during the writing of the book, and my daughter, Erika, proved a most valuable instructor for her daddy in her involvement with that most vital of all inventions of culture, the first. I am grateful, too, to Dick Cosme and Edward H. Stanford of Prentice-Hall for their patience and interest.

Like many other aspects of modern American interpretive culture, anthropology has developed the habit of preempting the means and idioms through which protest and contradiction are expressed and making them a part of its synthetic and culturally supportive message. Exoticism and cultural relativity are the bait, and the assumptions and ideologies of a Culture of collective enterprise are the hook that is swallowed with the bait. Anthropology is theorized and taught as an effort to *rationalize* contradiction, paradox, and dialectic, rather than to trace out and realize their implications; students and professionals alike learn to repress and ignore these implications, to "not see" them, and to imagine the most dire consequences as a putative result of not doing so. They repress the dialectic so that they may *be* it. I have written this book, with its explicit tracing out of the implications of relativity, as a determined effort to counteract this tendency in all of us.

Introduction

There are sciences whose "paradigms," blocks of theoretical precept and precedent that define the orthodoxy of what Thomas Kuhn calls "normal science," maintain a frozen immobility until their under-pinnings are melted by the heat and pressure of accumulated evidence, and a plate-tectonic revolution results. Anthropology is not one of these. As a discipline, anthropology has its history of theoretical devel-opment, of the ascendancy and antagonism of certain orientations, a history that, indeed, manifests a certain logic or order (which is dis-cussed in Chapter 6). For all the unanimity it commands, however, this flux of ideation might as well be described as a pure dialectic, a play of exposition (and denial) by disparate voices, or an eclectic accretion of all and sundry into the textbooks. What is remarkable about this is not so much the persistence of theoretical fossils (a per-sistance that is the stock-in-trade of academic tradition) but the failure of anthropology to institutionalize this persistence, or indeed, to in-stitutionalize a consensus at all.

If *The Invention of Culture* shows a tendency to assert its opinions, rather than arbitrate them, then this reflects, at least in part, the condition of a discipline in which a writer is obliged to distill his own tradition and his own consensus. Beyond this, the tendency relates to

some of the assumptions in the first three chapters and to the raison
d'être of the book.

A major concern of my argument is to analyze human motivation at a
radical level—one that cuts deeper than the very fashionable clichés
about the "interests" of corporations, political players, classes, "cal-
culating man," and so forth. This does not mean that I am blissfully and
naively unaware that such interests exist, or unconscious of the practical and ideological force of "interest" in the modern world. It means
that I would like to consider such interests as a subset, or surface
phenomenon, of more elemental questions. It would be, therefore
rather naive to expect a study of the cultural constitution of
phenomena to argue for "determination" of the process, or of
significant parts of it, by some particular, privileged phenomenal
context—especially when it argues that such contexts take their
significances largely from one another.

This, then, is the analytical standpoint of a book that elects to view
human phenomena from an "outside"—understanding that an outside
perspective is as readily created as our most reliable "inside" ones. The
discussion of cultural relativity is a case in point. Something of a red
herring for those who want to argue for the pervasiveness of socioeco-
nomic pressure, or against the possibility of a truly antiseptic scientific
objectivity, it has been introduced here in what appears to be a con-
troversially idealistic manner. But consider what is made of this
"idealism" in the ensuing discussion, where "culture" itself is presented
as a kind of illusion, a foil (and a kind of false objective) to aid the
anthropologist in arranging his experiences. It is, of course, possible
that the question of whether a false culture is truly or falsely relative has
some interest for the truly fastidious, but by and large the ordinary
premises for a vigorous, satisfying debate about "cultural relativity"
have been obviated.

The tendency to sidestep, to obviate, to "not deal with" many or most
of the chestnuts of theoretical hassling in anthropology, maddening as
it may be to those who have their terrain scouted and their land mines
set, is an artifact of the position I have taken. It is not, aside from this,
part of a willfull policy to rebuff anthropology or anthropologists, or to
beg spurious immunity for a privileged position. In choosing a new and
different terrain, I have merely exchanged one set of problems and
paradoxes for another, and the new set is every bit as formidable as the
old. A thorough examination of these problems would be helpful, as
would a marshalling of evidence for and against my position. But
arguments and evidence belong to a different level of investigation
(and, perhaps, of "science") than the one undertaken here.

This book was not written to prove, by evidence, argument, or example, any set of precepts or generalizations about human thought and action. It presents, simply, a different viewpoint for anthropologists, adumbrating the implications of this viewpoint for a number of areas of concern. If some or many of these implications fail to accord with some area of "observed fact," this is certainly because the model was deduced and extended outward, not built up by induction. Although it goes without saying that some deal of circumspection is crucial in model making of this sort, that the "rapport" is in the model, not the details, the procedure is ultimately that of Isaac Newton's famous dictum: "hypothesis non fingo." "I frame no hypotheses," the founder (and latterly, it seems, the "inventor") of exact science is reported to have said, indicating that he wrote his equations and deduced the world from them. I would add that the ability to see this as a humble, sober statement of procedure, rather than as vainglory, is a test of one's capacity for "outside" perspectives.

The theoretical diversity of anthropology makes it difficult to generalize critically about the field, however apt certain critical apprehensions of the drift of theorizing might be. Thus, although it seems that much of anthropological theorizing acknowledges cultural relativity simply in order to transform it into something else (not excepting the present symbolic theory), there have certainly been approaches (that of Franz Boas for instance) that do not do this. Again, the tendency, cataloged in my discussion of "The wax museum," to analogically discover (and evidentially confirm) gadgetries of computer programming and primitive cost-accounting, or grammars and dogmatics of social life, is, while still disturbingly rampant, certainly not universal in modern anthropology. I will acknowledge that a certain oversimplification in this respect, as well as others, may have resulted from my critical lumping together of certain approaches and has led to a wholly unintentional neglect of a number of promising directions and writers in anthropology.

Another point that may strike the reader as poor strategy, or perhaps as thoughtless perpetuation of an all-too-common error, is the opposition of Western conventionalism to the characteristic symbolic differentiation preferred by "traditional" peoples—including "tribal" societies, the ideologies of complex, stratified civilizations, and of certain classes in Western civil society. That the distinction is more involved than simplistic "progressive-conservative" dichotomies, aptly parodied by Marshall Sahlins as "the West and the Rest," should be evident from the discussion in Chapter 5. My argument, in brief, suggests that the differentiating mode of symbolization provides the only ideological regime capable of managing change. Nonstratified, decentralized peoples accommodate the collectivizing and differentiating sides of their cultural dialectic in an episodic alternation between ritual and secular states; highly developed civilizations secure the balance between these necessary halves of symbolic expression through the dialectical interaction of complementary social classes. In both instances it is sharp, decisive acts of differentiation—between sacred and secular, between class properties and prerogatives—that serve to regulate the whole. But modern Western society, which Louis Dumont accuses of "shamefaced stratification," is critically unbalanced: it suffers (or celebrates) differentiation as its "history" and counterbalances the marathon collectivism of its public enterprises with semiformal and shamefaced competitive ploys in all shades of gray, and with the desperate buffoonery of advertisement and entertainment. I would argue that we share with the Hellenistics of Alexandria, and with predialectic phases in other civilizations, a transient and highly unstable orientation. It is, however, part of a model, and most assuredly not a position assumed out of convenience.

In the inspiration and development of its theoretical program, *The Invention of Culture* represents a generalization of the argument in my monograph *Habu: The Innovation of Meaning in Daribi Religion* (Chicago 1972) and is an effort to situate his argument within the context of the symbolic constitution and motivation of actors in various cultural situations. Specifically, it builds upon the central idea of *Habu,* that all meaningful symbolizations compel the innovative and expressive force of tropes, or metaphors, because even conventional (referential) symbols, which we do not ordinarily think of as metaphors, have the effect of "innovating upon" (i.e., "being reflexively motivated as against") the extensions of their significances into other areas. Thus *Habu* derives cultural meaning from creative acts of innovative realization, building metaphor upon metaphor in such a way as to continually divert the force of earlier expressions and subsume it into newer constructions. The distinction between conventional, or collective, and individuating metaphors is not lost, however; it provides the axis between socializing (collective) and power-compelling (individuative) expressions. (In this respect the model resembles, and is doubtless indebted to, the discussion of "universalization and particularization" in Claude Lévi-Strauss's *The Savage Mind.*) Beyond this, the collective aspect of symbolization is also identified with the moral, or ethical, mode of culture, standing in a dialectical relation to that of the factual. (Cf. Clifford Geertz's essay "Ethos, World View, and the Analysis of Sacred Symbols" in *The Interpretation of Cultures.*)

As its epistemology, *The Invention of Culture* situates its argument *within* the *Habu* model and undertakes a radical exploration and development of the implications of the model. The series of interrelated and interlocking implications is presented in Chapter 3, and, despite the hazards of jargon in the necessary cross-referencing of special terms, it is presented "all at once."

The more significant additions to the *Habu* model include, first, a clarification of the contrasting effects of conventional and differentiating symbolization. As parts of the dialectic, they necessarily symbolize each other, but they do this in different ways. Conventional symbolization draws a contrast between the symbols themselves and the things they symbolize. I call this distinction, which works to distinguish the two modes in their respective ideological weightings, contextual contrast. Differentiating symbols assimilate or encompass the things they symbolize. I call this effect, which always works to negate the distinction between the modes, to collapse them, or derive one from the other, obviation. Since these effects are reflexive (i.e., that which "is symbolized" works its effect, in turn, upon that which symbolizes), all symbolic effects are mobilized in any act of symbolization. Hence, the second addition, is that the awareness of the symbolizer must be concentrated upon one of the modes at any given time. Focusing attention upon this "control," the symbolizer perceives the opposite mode as something quite different, an internal "compulsion" or "motivation." The third addition is that every "culture," or significant cultural class, will favor one symbolic modality as the area appropriate to human action and regard the other as manifesting the "given" or "innate" world. Chapter 4 explores the significance of this for human motivational and personality structure, and Chapter 5 develops a model of cultural integration and evolution based on contextual contrast and obviation.

The "episodic" operation of the dialectic in tribal or acephalous societies is, except for its theoretical underpinnings, closely parallel to the model of balanced symmetrical and complementary schismogenesis presented by Gregory Bateson in "Epilogue 1936" of his book *Naven*. This doubtless reflects my familiarity with, and admiration for, Bateson's work. Less obvious is the inadvertent similarity between Dumont's homo hierarchicus/homo aequalis contrast and the pointed comparisions I make between "relativized" modern American society and the dialectically balanced social orders of older civilizations. The dialectic of social classes envisioned here owes most perhaps to Dumont and to David M. Schneider and Raymond T. Smith's remarkable *Class Differences and Sex Roles in American Kinship and Family Structure*.

The notion of a cultural dynamic based on the mediation of realms of human responsibility (and nonresponsibility) is less easily traceable to other sources. The issue has received further treatment in my article "Scientific and Indigenous Papuan Conceptualisations of the Innate" (see Bayless-Smith and Feachem, eds., *Subsistence and Survival* [Academic Press 1977]) and in Dr. Marilyn Strathern's "No Nature, No Culture: The Hagen Case" (forthcoming). My book *Lethal Speech: Daribi Myth as Symbolic Obviation* (Cornell 1978) carries the point further in its development of the radical implications of obviation, as the extended, or processual form of trope. *Lethal Speech* is "about" obviation, as indeed *Habu* is about metaphor, and *The Invention of Culture,* concerned as it is with the relation of these forms to convention, thus becomes the middle term of an unintended trilogy.

My use of the term "invention" here is, I think, much more traditional than contemporary "bolt-from-the-blue" stereotypes of lucky cavemen and accidental discoveries. Like invention in music, it refers to a positive and expected component of human life. The term seems to have retained much of this same sense from the time of the Roman rhetoricians through the dawn of early modern philosophy. In the *Dialectical Invention* of the fifteenth-century humanist Rudolphus Agricola, invention appears as one of the "parts" of the dialectic, finding or proposing an analogy for a *propositus* that can then be "judged" in reaching a conclusion—rather in the manner in which a scientific hypothesis is subject to the judgment of "testing."

Invention being largely undetermined for the ancients as well as the medieval philosophers, it fell to the mechanistic-materialist world view, with its Newtonian determinism, to banish it to the realm of "accident." Beyond this, of course, there is the inevitable temptation to co-opt accident itself (i.e., entropy, the measure, *please,* not of randomness, but of our ignorance!) into the "system," to trace its blind fencing with "necessity" in evolutionary studies, to play the "life-insurance game" with subatomic particles, to write the grammar of metaphor or the braille of nonverbal communication, or to program computers to write blank verse (almost as badly, at times, as human beings have been known to do). But co-opting, or predicating, invention and dealing satisfactorily with it are two rather different matters.

There was a certain inevitability, in any event, to the encounter between the anthropology of symbols and the "black hole" of modern symbolic theory—the "negative symbol," the trope, which generates (or obliges one to invent) its own referents. *The Invention of Culture* appeared in print at roughly the same time as three other, remarkably different soundings of the black hole: D. Sperber's *Rethinking Sym-*

bolism, Fredrik Barth's *Ritual and Knowledge among the Baktaman,* and Carlos Castaneda's *Tales of Power.* For Sperber, the black hole is not so much a gravity well as an obscuring dust cloud. It amounts to the place where reference stops; "knowledge" is achieved in the formation of a metaphor, but it is a knowledge forged on a personal level in imitation of a more broadly held "encyclopedic" (i.e., conventional) knowledge. Sperber understands perfectly well that a metaphor presents a challenge, that one must, as Casteneda's confidants would have it, "win the knowledge for oneself." But the result, to judge from his conclusions, is more a counterfeit than an invention. Invention cannot reveal, and thereby create, the world for Sperber as it can for Piaget, because it plays such a poor second to "real" knowledge.

Baktaman culture, in Barth's account, is very nearly the opposite of this. Although he tacitly admits that meaning is constituted through metaphor, the metaphor, in the utter absence of shared assumptions or associations, is built upon shared sensations—the dew upon the grass, the redness of pandanus fruit, and so forth—in a kind of "dumb barter" of semiological tokens. Conventional signs, far from attaining currency through the continual reshuffling of metaphors, are swallowed up in the secrecy of their formation, and what "knowledge" there may be is hoarded and confided in driblets to initiates. Like radio messages sent between black holes, very little gets through. Even granting Barth a modicum of rhetorical license for exaggeration, however, one is forced to ask, amid such hermetically sealed vacuums of self-interested noncommunication, just whom the Baktaman think they are keeping their secrets from.

After all that has been written about the conjectural sources of Castaneda's writings, all that one can do is extend to them the same professional suspension of disbelief one would grant to an ethnographer reporting on some exotic African or Far-Eastern belief system. The exquisitely self-contained and dialectical model presented in *Tales of Power* looks like a "Buddhist" rejoinder to the "Hinduism" of the Aztec theology of Moyucoyani (the god who "invented himself," from the Nahuatl verb *yucoyo,* "to invent") described by Leon-Portilla. But even if Castaneda had "invented" the whole thing himself, the timeliness of this exemplar of the anthropology of symbols would be significant. For the *nagual* (power, "that with which we do not deal"), in its opposition to the *tonal* ("everything that can be named," convention), is the cleanest expression of the negative symbol that we have. It is the thing that *makes* metaphor but always escapes in its expression. (And here it might be helpful to recall that the Middle-American cultures share with the Indian culture the distinction of having independently originated the symbol of the zero, the "negative quantity.")

I have, with evident bias, discussed these three contemporaries of *The Invention of Culture,* not because of any failings or advantages they may have, but because, for all their differences of approach or epistemology, they comprehend the properties of the negative symbol in precisely the same way. The differences arise in what is made of these properties and how their relation to conventional symbols is effected. To treat invention as symbolism manqué, to regard it as spurious knowledge, as Sperber does, is to subvert the most powerful thing there is for the afflatus of a knowledge-proud civilization. To treat it, as Barth does, as a true "black hole," invention that devours convention, is, while admittedly a superb demonstration of the tendency of negative symbolization, a kind of abdication of the human situation. One might, indeed, contrast Sperber and Barth as "subjective objectivism" and "objective subjectivism," respectively.

The dialectical approach, by contrast, subverts subjectivity and objectivity alike in the interests of mediation. Its stance, which has proven to be by turns maddeningly frustrating and tantalizingly obscure to critics of this book, is to assert some disquietingly subversive things about conventional knowledge, and some implausibly positive ones about nonconventional operations. Castaneda's practice of this mediation, with its bizarre adventures among moths and acrobatic shamans, is in the service of an enlightenment as seductive and as practically unattainable as the Zen *satori.* Anthropology has traditionally set its sights somewhat lower, making a little *satori* go a long way. But the problems of following "the meanings made under the order of the tonal" are not without their contaminating effects on one's prose style as well as one's model.

Returning, then, to the issue of how my arguments are situated within the realm of theoretical discourse: the grave danger, especially given the abstract discussion of "culture" at the outset, is that some readers will want to align my position on the idealist/pragmatist axis. Like the phenomenologists and ethnomethodologists and *some* Marxist anthropologists, however, my stance has been to sidestep, to analyze, or to circumvent this axis, rather than to take up a position with respect to it. This means that, despite whatever analogies one might find with Alfred Schütz, with philosophical "construction of reality" models, or with the "synthetic a priori" of Immanuel Kant, this work is not "philosophical," and it is not philosophy. It eschews, in fact, the ethnocentric "Questions" and points of orientation that philosophy deems so necessary in supporting (and defending) its idealism. But it also means that, despite the important idiom of "production" in the second chapter, I have no interest in "left-flanking" movements that would bring the "realities" of hard-nosed production into the stale fora of academic discourse. Realities, Chapter 3 seems to tell us, are what we make them, not what they make us, or what they make us do.

Finally, since I *do* seem to be interested in symbols, some clarification on this much-belabored topic is in order. As should be evident from the exposition in the later chapters, I do not aspire (except, perhaps, conceptually) to a "linguage" that would talk about symbols, symbols-in-discourse, etc.. more accurately, more precisely, or more fully than they "talk about themselves." A science of symbols would seem to be as inadvisable as such other quixotic attempts to state the unstateable as a grammer of metaphor or an absolute dictionary. That is because symbols and people exist in a mediating relationship to one another—they are our besetting devils as we are theirs—and the question of whether "collectivizing" and "differentiating" are ultimately symbolic or human dispositions becomes hopelessly entangled in the toils of the mediation.

Have I, then, artificially exaggerated the polarities of human symbolization by imposing extreme contrasts and oppositions upon usages that are most often only relatively opposable, and even then debatably so? Of course I have, hoping that, like the tracery of semivisible geometry that Cezanne introduced into his landscapes, this "imagery" would help us see the landscape better. Has this concerto for symbols and percussion too many notes, as was once said of Mozart's music? Of course it has, and I would rather listen to Mozart.

Having by now completed what is largely the function of these introductions, which is to tell the reader what the book is not, we might consider the perennially "relevant" question of Lenin: what is to be done? Is a true anthropology like that envisaged by Kant and Jean-Paul Sartre, possible, or any nearer to realization than when I wrote this book? Perhaps. But since anthropology, like most other modern enterprises, is largely "about" itself, the better question would be, what would such an ideally constituted anthropology produce? (And the answer, of course, is "more anthropology.") What, then, of the possibility of achieving a truly dialectical balance in Western society, of obviating the hopeless wastage of ideological and motivational canards and the "quantity for quantity's sake" (this means "economic mobilization for its own sake") of this miasma of warfare states? Apart from the fact that it will take care of itself (in what apalling ways we can only guess), the question of global improvement calls to mind the plight of a Chinese poet. He lived in that great, sleepy time when Confucius and the *tao* had taken care of China's spiritual discords, and the mandarins took care of everything else. And he would wistfully imagine, when he saw a great cloud of dust rise against the horizon, that it was "the dust of a thousand chariots." It never was. We live in interesting times.

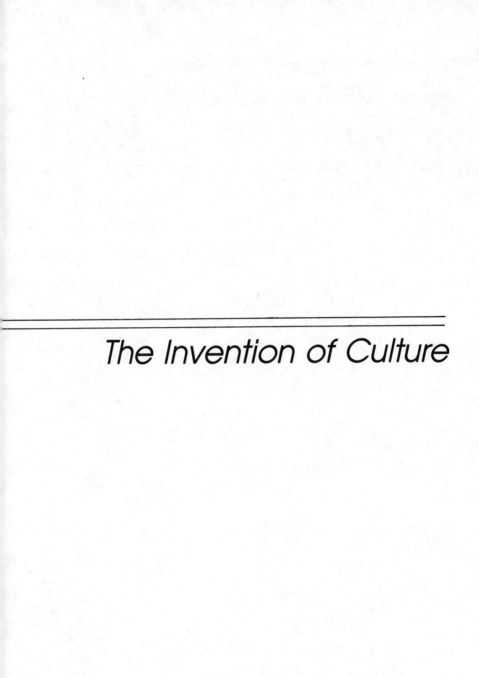

The Invention of Culture

chapter 1

The assumption of culture

The idea of culture

Anthropology studies the phenomenon of man, not simply man's mind, his body, evolution, origins, tools, art, or groups alone, but as parts or aspects of a general pattern, or whole. To emphasize this fact and make it a part of their ongoing effort, anthropologists have brought a general word into widespread use to stand for the phenomenon, and that word is *culture*. When they speak as if there were only one culture, as in "human culture," this refers very broadly to the phenomenon of man; otherwise, in speaking of "a culture" or "the cultures of Africa," the reference is to specific historical and geographical traditions, special cases of the phenomenon of man. Thus culture has become a way of talking about man, and about particular instances of man, when viewed from a certain perspective. Of course the word "culture" has other connotations as well, and important ambiguities which we shall examine presently.

By and large, though, the concept of culture has come to be so completely associated with anthropological thinking that if we should ever want to, we could define an anthropologist as someone who uses the word "culture" habitually. Or else, since the process of coming to depend on this concept is generally something of a "conversion

1

experience," we might want to amend this somewhat and say that an anthropologist is someone who uses the word "culture" with hope—or even with faith.

The perspective of the anthropologist is an especially grand and far-reaching one, for the phenomenon of man implies a comparison with the other phenomena of the universe, with animal societies and living species, with the fact of life, matter and space, and so forth. The term "culture," too, in its broadest sense, attempts to bring man's actions and meanings down to the most basic level of significance, to examine them in universal terms in an attempt to understand them. When we speak of people belonging to different cultures, then, we are referring to a very basic kind of difference between them, suggesting that there are specific varieties of the phenomenon of man. Although there has been much "inflation" of the word "culture," it is in this "strong" sense that I will use it here.

The fact that anthropology chooses to study man in terms that are at the same time so broad and so basic, to understand both man's uniqueness and his diversity through the notion of culture, poses a peculiar situation for the science. Like the epistemologist, who considers "the meaning of meaning," or like the psychologist, who thinks about how people think, the anthropologist is forced to include himself and his own way of life in his subject matter, and study himself. More accurately, since we speak of a person's total capability as "culture," the anthropologist uses his own culture to study others, and to study culture in general.

Thus the awareness of culture brings about an important qualification of the anthropologist's aims and viewpoint as a scientist: the classical rationalist's pretense of absolute objectivity must be given up in favor of a relative objectivity based on the characteristics of one's own culture. It is necessary, of course, for a research worker to be as unbiased as possible insofar as he is aware of his assumptions, but we often take our culture's more basic assumptions so much for granted that we are not even aware of them. Relative objectivity can be achieved through discovering what these tendencies are, the ways in which one's culture allows one to comprehend another, and the limitations it places on this comprehension. "Absolute" objectivity would require that the anthropologist have no biases, and hence no culture at all.

The idea of culture, in other words, places the researcher in a position of equality with his subjects: each "belongs to a culture." Because every culture can be understood as a specific manifestation, or example, of the phenomenon of man, and because no infallible method has ever been discovered for "grading" different cultures and sorting them into their natural types, we assume that every culture, as such, is equivalent to every other one. This assumption is called "cultural relativity."

The combination of these two implications of the idea of culture, the fact that we ourselves belong to a culture (relative objectivity), and that we must assume all cultures to be equivalent (cultural relativity), leads to a general proposition concerning the study of culture. As the repetition of the stem "relative" suggests, the understanding of another culture involves the relationship between two varieties of the human phenomenon; it aims at the creation of an intellectual relation between them, an understanding that includes both of them. The idea of "relationship" is important here because it is more appropriate to the bringing together of two equivalent entities, or viewpoints, than notions like "analysis" or "examination," with their pretensions of absolute objectivity.

Let us take a closer look at the way in which this relation is achieved. An anthropologist *experiences*, in one way or another, the subject of his study; he does so through the world of his own meanings, and then uses this meaningful experience to communicate an understanding to those of his own culture. He can only communicate this understanding if his account makes sense in the terms of his culture. And yet if these theories and discoveries represent uncontrolled fantasies, like many of the anecdotes of Herodotus, or the travelers' tales of the Middle Ages, we can scarcely speak of a proper relating of cultures. An "anthropology" which never leaves the boundaries of its own conventions, which disdains to invest its imagination in a world of experience, must always remain more an ideology than a science.

But here the question arises of how much experience is necessary. Must the anthropologist be adopted into a tribe, get on familiar terms with chiefs and kings, or marry into an average family? Need he only view slides, study maps, and interview captives? Optimally, of course, one would want to know as much as possible about one's subjects, but in practice the answer to this question depends upon how much time and money are available, and on the scope and intentions of the undertaking. For the quantitative researcher, the archeologist dealing with evidences of a culture, or the sociologist measuring its effects, the problem is one of obtaining an adequate *sample*, finding enough evidential material so that one's estimates are not too far off. But the cultural or social anthropologist, although he may at times be concerned with sampling, is committed to a different kind of thoroughness—one based on the depth and comprehensiveness of his insight into the subject culture.

If the thing that anthropologists call "culture" is as all-encompass-

ing as we have assumed, then this obsession on the part of the fieldworker is not misplaced, for the subject culture is as much a separate
world of thought and action as his own. The only way in which a
researcher could possibly go about the job of creating a relation between such entities would be to simultaneously *know* both of them, to
realize the relative character of his own culture through the concrete
formulation of another. Thus gradually, in the course of fieldwork, he
himself becomes the link between cultures through his living in both
of them, and it is this "knowledge" and competence that he draws
upon in describing and explaining the subject culture. "Culture" in
this sense draws an invisible equal sign between the knower (who
comes to know himself) and the known (who are a community of
knowers).

We might actually say that an anthropologist "invents" the culture
he believes himself to be studying, that the relation is more "real" for
being his particular acts and experiences than the things it "relates."
Yet this explanation is only justified if we understand the invention
to take place objectively, along the lines of observing and learning,
and not as a kind of free fantasy. In experiencing a new culture, the
fieldworker comes to realize new potentialities and possibilities for the
living of life, and may in fact undergo a personality change himself.
The subject culture becomes "visible," and then "believable" to him,
he apprehends it first as a distinct entity, a way of doing things, and
then secondly as a way in which he could be doing things. Thus he
comprehends for the first time, through the intimacy of his own
mistakes and triumphs, what anthropologists speak of when they use
the word "culture." Before this he had no culture, as we might say,
since the culture in which one grows up is never really "visible"—it is
taken for granted, and its assumptions are felt to be self-evident. It is
only through "invention" of this kind that the abstract significance of
culture (and of many another concept) can be grasped, and only
through the experienced contrast that his own culture becomes
"visible." In the act of inventing another culture, the anthropologist
invents his own, and in fact he reinvents the notion of culture itself.

Making culture visible

In spite of all he may have been told about fieldwork, in spite of all
the descriptions of other cultures and other fieldworkers' experiences
he may have read, the anthropologist first arriving among the people
he will study is apt to feel lonely and helpless. He may or may not
know something about the people he has arrived to work among, he

may perhaps even be able to speak their language, but the fact remains that as a person he must start from scratch. It is as a person, then, as a participant, that his invention of the subject culture begins. He has heretofore experienced "culture" as an academic abstraction, a thing allegedly so diverse and multifaceted, yet monolithic, that it is difficult to grasp or visualize. But as long as he cannot "see" this culture in his surroundings, it is of little use or comfort to him.

The immediate problems facing the beginning fieldworker are not likely to be academic or intellectual; they are practical, and they have a definite cause. Disoriented and dazed as he may be, he often encounters a good deal of trouble in getting settled and making contacts. If a house is being built for him, all sorts of delays occur in the work; if he hires assistants or interpreters, they fail to show up. When he complains about delays and desertions the usual lame excuses are offered. His questions may be answered by obvious and deliberate lies. Dogs bark at him and children may follow him about in the streets. All these circumstances stem from the fact that people are usually uncomfortable with a stranger in their midst, more especially with an outsider who may be crazy, dangerous, or both. Often they create difficulties for him as "defenses," to keep him at a distance or at least stall him off while he is considered and examined more closely.

These delays, defenses, and other ways of putting off the fieldworker are neither necessarily hostile (though they may be) nor unique in human interaction. "Distance" of this sort is a common occurrence in the beginning stages of what might possibly become a close personal involvement, such as a friendship or a love affair, and it is commonly pointed out that too much familiarity at this point would tend to undermine the mutual respect of the parties concerned. However this may be, human beings in all societies are usually more perceptive than we give them credit for, and life in a small community is generally far more intimate than the newcomer imagines. Courtesy, an age-old "solution" to the problems of human encounter, has made situations of this sort the basis of a high art, and the kindest thing a distraught fieldworker can do is at least suspect his hosts of courtesy.

However much these first encounters are jarred by misunderstanding, masked by formalities, or cushioned by courtesies, they nevertheless must take place, for the simple facts of being human and being in a place generate certain dependencies on their own account. Thus it is often the most trivial and ludicrous occasions, like looking for a place to relieve oneself, trying to operate a stove, or dealing with the landlord, that form the bulk of a beginner's social relations. In fact, these occasions offer the only available "bridge" for empathy between stranger and native; they "humanize" the former, making his problems so readily understandable that anybody could sympathize with them. And yet the laughter and warmth that comes so easily on these occasions can never be a substitute for the more intimate and pene-trating companionship and understanding that are such an important part of life in any culture. A relationship which is based on simplify-ing oneself to the barest essentials has nowhere to go—unless one is willing to permanently adopt the role of village idiot.

Whether or not he finds these initial encounters satisfying, the fieldworker will nevertheless try to follow them up and build them into more substantial friendships. He will do this because he is lonely, perhaps, or because he knows that if he is to learn something about these people and their way of life, he will have to learn it from them. For casual acquaintance is the accepted prelude to closer relationship in all human societies. But as soon as he attempts anything more ambitious than simple pleasantries, he begins to experience contradic-tions in his basic expectations of how people should conduct their affairs. This will not involve things as abstract as "ideas" or "points of view," at least not at this stage, but ordinary notions of "common decency," and perhaps subliminal effects that tend to make one vaguely uncomfortable, such as physical closeness, rapidity of movement, ges-tures, and so on. Should the well-meaning stranger, perhaps feeling guilty because of the "mistakes" he has already made, redouble his efforts at friendship, he will only succeed in compounding his diffi-culties further. Perhaps, as in many small communities, the ties of friendship are so encompassing that a "friend" is expected to fit into the roles of confidant, kinsman, creditor, and business partner all at once; possibly there are excessive reciprocal expectations, or a kind of "one-upmanship" hospitality, or even strong feelings about the soli-darity of friends in factional disputes.

These initial frustrations can be expected to build up, for the pat-tern for friendship is often repeated in many other particulars of social life. Gradually the fieldworker begins to feel his effectiveness as a per-son undermined, and it is small consolation to know that the local people may be "humoring" the stranger, or trying to make life easy for him. Better an honest mistake than a false conviviality. Even the most tolerant and well-meaning outsider, who keeps his own counsel and strives to avoid showing his frustration eventually finds the strain of trying to maintain his own thoughts and expectations while "re-specting" those of the local people extremely wearing. He may feel inadequate, or perhaps suspect that he has allowed his ideals of toler-ance and relativity to trap him in a situation that is beyond his control.

This feeling is known to anthropologists as "culture shock." In it the local "culture" first manifests itself to the anthropologist through his own *inadequacy;* against the backdrop of his new surroundings it is he who has become "visible." The situation has some parallels within our own society: the freshman first entering college, the new army recruit, and anyone else who is compelled to live in "new" or alien surroundings, all have had some taste of this kind of "shock." Typically the sufferer is depressed and anxious, he may withdraw into himself, or grasp at any chance to communicate with others. To a degree that we seldom realize, we depend upon the participation of others in our lives, and upon our own participation in the lives of others. Our success and effectiveness as persons is based upon this participation, and upon an ability to maintain a controlling competence in communicating with others. Culture shock is a loss of the self through the loss of these supports. College freshmen and army recruits, who find themselves, after all, in another segment of their own culture, soon establish some control over the situation. For the anthropological fieldworker, however, the problem is both more pressing and more enduring.

The problem also exists, though not exactly in the same way, for the people the anthropologist has come to work among. They are faced with an odd, prying, curious-looking, and strangely naive outsider in their midst, one who, like a child, keeps asking questions and must be taught everything, and who, also like a child, is apt to get into trouble. In spite of the defenses that have been erected against him, he remains an object of curiosity and often fear, fitting many of the rather ambiguous stereotypes of the "dangerous" outsider, or perhaps the conniving Westerner. The community may experience a mild "shock" of its own—perhaps we ought to call it "anthropologist shock" —and become self-conscious about its doings.[1] It finds "control" an important problem, too. But the community's problem is not the anthropologist's problem of managing personal competence in dealing with others. The community's problem is simply controlling the anthropologist.

The solution for all concerned lies in the anthropologist's efforts to control his culture shock, to deal with the frustration and helplessness of his initial situation. Since his control involves acquiring a competence in the local language and ways of life (and who but the natives are experts in this?), the local people are given a chance to do

---

1. Thus the Reverend Kenneth Mesplay, who was in charge of a mission school and other services at Karimui, where I did my fieldwork, claims that villages where an anthropologist has lived show distinctive patterns in dealing with Europeans. School attendance drops off, the people show more self-assurance, etc. An anthropologist is something of a "culture missionary," believing (like all good missionaries) in the thing he invents, and is apt to acquire a substantial local following in his efforts to invent the local culture.

their part in controlling the outsider, domesticating him, as it were. And here is where the anthropologist's experiences differ from those of missionaries and other emissaries of Western society. The latter are often compelled by their chosen roles and apprehensions of the situation either to interpret their shortcomings as personal inadequacy—and go crazy—or as native cussedness and slovenliness, thus reinforcing their own elitist self-images.

But anthropology teaches us to objectify the thing we are adjusting to as "culture," much as the psychoanalyst or shaman exorcises the patient's anxieties by objectifying their source. Once the new situation has been objectified as "culture," it is possible to say that the field-worker is "learning" that culture, the way one might learn a card game. On the other hand, since the objectification takes place simultaneously with the learning, it could as well be said that the field-worker is "inventing" the culture.

The distinction is a crucial one, though, from the standpoint of how an anthropologist comes to understand and explain the situation he experiences. The fieldworker's belief that the new situation he is dealing with is a concrete entity, a "thing" that has rules, "works" in a certain way, and can be learned, will help and encourage him in his attempts to come to grips with it. And yet in a very important sense he is *not* learning the culture the way a child would, for he approaches the situation already an adult who has effectively internalized his own culture. His efforts to understand the subjects of his research, to make them and their ways meaningful, and to communicate this meaningfulness to others, will grow out of his abilities to make meaning within his own culture. Whatever he "learns" from his subjects will therefore take the form of an extension or superstructure, built upon that which he already knows, and built *of* that which he already knows. He will "participate" in the subject culture, not in the way a native does, but as someone who is simultaneously enveloped in his own world of meanings, *and these meanings will also participate.* If we recall what was said earlier about relative objectivity, we remember it is the set of cultural predispositions that an outsider brings with him that makes all the difference in his understanding of what is "there."

If culture were an absolute, objective "thing," then "learning" it would be the same for all people, native as well as outsider, adult as well as child. But people have all sorts of predispositions and biases, and the notion of culture as an objective, inflexible entity can only be useful as a sort of "prop" to aid the anthropologist in his invention and understanding. For this, and for many other purposes in anthropology, it is necessary to proceed *as if* culture existed as some monolithic "thing," but for the purpose of demonstrating how it is that an anthropologist attains his comprehension of another people, it is necessary to realize that culture is a "prop."

The relation that the anthropologist builds between two cultures—which, in turn, objectifies and hence "creates" those cultures for him—arises precisely from his act of "invention," his use of meanings known to him in constructing an understandable representation of his subject matter. The result is an analogy, or a set of analogies, that "translates" one group of basic meanings into the other, and can be said to participate in both meaning systems at the same time in the same way that their creator does. This is the simplest, most basic, and most important consideration of all; the anthropologist cannot simply "learn" the new culture and place it beside the one he already knows, but must rather "take it on" so as to experience a transformation of his own world. "Going native" is as unprofitable from the standpoint of fieldwork as staying at the airport or hotel and making up stories about the natives; in neither case is there any possibility of a meaningful relation (and invention) of cultures. It is naive to suggest that going native is the only way to really "learn" another culture, since this would necessitate giving up one's own. Thus, since every effort to know another culture must at least begin with an act of invention, the would-be native could only enter a world of his own creation, like a schizophrenic or that apocryphal Chinese painter who, pursued by creditors, painted a goose on the wall, mounted it, and flew away!

Culture is made visible by culture-shock, by subjecting oneself to situations beyond one's normal interpersonal competence and objectifying the discrepancy as an entity; it is delineated through an inventive realization of that entity following the initial experience. For the anthropologist this delineation usually proceeds along the lines of anthropological expectations of what culture and cultural difference should be. Once the realization occurs, the fieldworker acquires a heightened awareness of the kinds of differences and similarities implied by the term "culture," and he begins to use it more and more as an explanatory construct. He begins to see his own way of life in sharp relief against the background of the other "cultures" he knows, and he may try consciously to objectify it (although it is "there," by implication at least, in the analogies he has already created). Thus the invention of cultures, and of culture in general, often begins with the invention of one particular culture, and this, by the process of invention, both is and is not the inventor's own.

The peculiar situation of the anthropological fieldworker, participating simultaneously in two distinct worlds of meaning and action, requires that he relate to his research subjects as an "outsider," trying to "learn" and penetrate their way of life, while relating to his own culture as a kind of metaphorical "native." To both groups he is a professional stranger, a person who holds himself aloof from their lives in order to gain perspective. This "strangeness" and the "in-between" character of the anthropologist has been the cause of many misunderstandings and exaggerations on the part of those he comes into contact with. Those of his own society imagine he has "gone native," whereas the natives often feel he is a spy or a government agent. Troublesome as these suspicions may be, they are outweighed by the impact of his situation on the anthropologist himself. Insofar as he functions as a "bridge" or point of relation between two ways of life, he creates for himself an illusion of transcending them. This point accounts for much of the power anthropology has over its converts, its evangelistic message: it draws people who want to emancipate themselves from their culture.

Emancipation may indeed follow, less from the fact that the fieldworker has made good his "escape" than from the circumstance that he has found a powerful new "control" on his invention. The relation that he creates binds the inventor quite as much as it binds the "cultures" that he invents. The experience of culture, endowed with the very formidable reality of the difficulties involved, lends a sureness to his thinking and feeling that confirmed belief seems always to afford its adherents.

The invention of culture

Anthropology is the study of man "as if" there were culture. It is brought into being by the invention of culture, both in the general sense, as a concept, and in the specific sense, through the invention of particular cultures. Since anthropology exists through the idea of culture, this has become its overall idiom, a way of talking about, understanding, and dealing with things, and it is incidental to ask whether cultures exist. They exist through the fact of their being invented, and through the effectiveness of this invention.

This invention need not take place in the course of fieldwork; it can be said to occur whenever and wherever some "alien" or "foreign" set of conventions is brought into relation with one's own. Fieldwork is a particularly instructive example because it develops the relation out of the field situation and its ensuing personal problems. But many anthropologists never do fieldwork, and for many who do, fieldwork is just a special instance (although a highly instructive one) of the invention of culture. This invention, in turn, is part of the more general phenomenon of human creativity—it transforms the mere assumption of culture into a creative art.

An anthropologist calls the situation he is studying "culture" first of all so that he can *understand* it in familiar terms, so he knows how to deal with and control his experience. But he also does so in order to see what calling this situation "culture" does to his understanding of culture in general. Whether he knows it or not, and whether he intends it or not, his "safe" act of making the strange familiar always makes the familiar a little bit strange. And the more familiar the strange becomes, the more and more strange the familiar will appear. It is a kind of game, if you will, a game of pretending that the ideas and conventions of other peoples are the same (in one broadly conceived way or another) as our own so that we can see what happens when we "play" our own concepts through the lives and actions of others. As the anthropologist uses the notion of culture to control his field experiences, those experiences will, in turn, come to control his notion of culture. He invents "a culture" for people, and *they* invent "culture" for him.

Once the fieldworker's experience is organized around culture and controlled by it, his invention will retain a meaningful relation to our own mode of life and thought. Thus it comes to embody a kind of metamorphosis, an effort of continued, ongoing change in our culture's forms and possibilities brought about by a concern with the understanding of other peoples. We cannot use analogies to reveal the idiosyncrasies of other life styles without applying the latter, as "controls," in the rearticulation of our own. Anthropological understanding becomes an "investment" of our ideas and our way of life in the broadest sense possible, and the gains to be realized have correspondingly far-reaching implications. The "Culture" we live is threatened, criticized, counterexemplified by the "cultures" we create—and vice versa.

The study or representation of another culture is no more a mere "description" of the subject matter than a painting "describes" the thing it depicts. In both cases there is a symbolization, one that is connected with the anthropologist's or artist's intention to represent the subject in the first place. And yet the creator cannot be conscious of this symbolic intent in pursuing the details of his invention, for that would nullify the guiding effect of his "control," and thus make his invention self-conscious. A self-conscious anthropological study or work of art is one that is manipulated by its author to the point where it says exactly what he wanted it to say, and excludes that kind of extension or self-transformation that we call "learning" or "expression."

Thus our understanding needs the external, the objective, whether this be technique itself, as in "nonobjective" art, or palpable research subjects. By forcing his imagination, through analogy, to follow the detailed conformations of some external and unpredictable subject, the scientist's or artist's invention gains a sureness it would not otherwise command. Invention is "controlled" by the image of reality and the creator's lack of awareness that he is creating. His imagination, and often his whole management of himself, is compelled to come to grips with a new situation; it is frustrated, as in culture shock, in its initial intention, and so brought to invent a solution.

What the fieldworker invents, then, is his own understanding; the analogies he creates are extensions of his own notions and those of his culture, transformed by his experiences of the field situation. He uses the latter as a kind of "lever," the way a pole vaulter uses his pole, to catapult his comprehension beyond the limitations imposed by earlier viewpoints. If he intends his analogies to be no analogies at all, but an objective description of the culture, he will make every effort to refine them into a closer and closer approximation of his experience. Where he finds discrepancies between his own invention and the native "culture" as he comes to know it, he changes and reworks his invention until its analogies seem more appropriate or "accurate." If this process is prolonged, as it is in the course of fieldwork, the anthropologist's use of the idea of "culture" will eventually assume a sophisticated and articulate form. Gradually the subject, the objectified element that serves as a "control" for his invention, is invented through analogies incorporating progressively more comprehensive articulations, so that a set of impressions is re-created as a set of meanings.

The effect of this invention is as profound as it is unconscious; it creates the subject in the act of trying to represent it more objectively, and simultaneously creates (through analogous extension) the ideas and forms through which it is invented. The "control," whether subject culture or artist's model, forces the representer to live up to his impressions of it, yet those impressions themselves change as he becomes more and more absorbed in his task. A good artist or scientist becomes a detached part of his culture, one that grows in strange new ways, and carries its ideas through transformations that others may never experience. This is why artists can be called "educators"; we have something—a development of our thoughts—to learn from them. And this is why it is worthwhile studying other peoples, because every understanding of another culture is an experiment with our own.

In fact, the subjects of study that we pursue in the arts and sciences can be seen as "controls" on the creation of our culture. Our "learning" and "development" always carry forward the meaningful articulation and movement of the ideas that provide our orientation. As an example, and a "control" on a discussion that has necessarily tended toward abstraction, let us consider the work of an artist who took such an interest in man in general and his life styles that he might almost be called an anthropologist: the Flemish painter Peter Bruegel the elder.

As with all historical examples, the background of Bruegel's life and work was complex, with many cross-cutting influences, and a simplification is necessary to any discussion. In artistic terms, a most important consideration is the tradition of painting that grew up in the Low Countries and the Duchy of Burgundy from the early 1400s onwards, which contrasted with, and sometimes fed upon, the renaissance art of Italy. The early masters of this Flemish school, among them Jan van Eyck, Rogier van der Weyden, and Hans Memlinc, developed a style of depiction based on perspective, graphic realism, and intensive detail. The force of this art was its realization of idealized religious scenes and subjects in the most convincing forms possible; each picture is a study in intricacy. The crucifixion, the Virgin and Child, and other themes were given "life" and immediacy through the artist's uncanny control over the "look" and "feel" of familiar objects: the gleam of light on polished metal, the folds of skin or fabric, or the precise outlines of leaves or branches.

As this general style became established, it provided a basis for further development. Its uncanny command of detail and convincing ability to counterfeit reality increased enormously the range of invention possible to the artist. Whereas painters of the early and middle 1400s enriched their own (and their countrymen's) understanding of the Gospel by recreating it in reality, their successors used this technique to study (and broaden) their entire world view. Hieronymus Bosch mastered a whole genre by merging the realism of Flemish painting with fantastic allegories of the human condition. His pictures of vermin and birds in men's clothing, atrocities, and weirdly juxtaposed objects *use* the realism of the earlier masters as a means of stark caricature. It was in this form, the most extreme possible, that character and moral differentiation were introduced into the realm of realistic depiction.

The art of Peter Bruegel constituted an analogous, though rather different, departure from the earlier realism. Bruegel's works retained the force of allegory, including the irony of treating profane subjects in intricate detail, but he tempered his caricature. Much more than Bosch, who generally relied on the fantastic, the caricature and symbolic irony of Bruegel's works is achieved through the detailed portrayal of Flemish peasants and their folkways. The contrast between this subject matter, depicted with a penetrating characterization that implies long observation, and the themes Bruegel chose to illustrate, creates an irony and an explanatory force not unlike that of anthropology, which also objectifies its insights through the folkways of others. In both cases the life of the people is described, explained, made plausible; but in the process the whole work comes to mean something more than the mere description or understanding of a people.

Bruegel was fascinated, as his sketches show, with the circumstances of life among the peasants of his country; their clothing, their houses, their habits and amusements. He took an artist's delight in the geometry of their forms, accentuated by the postures characteristic of their labor or merriment, and harmonized his total compositions with a fine sense of the intimacy between peasant and landscape. The significance of this superb artistic penetration of folkways is evident in another fascination of the artist: his obsession with proverb and allegory. Proverb and peasantry are indeed two aspects of the same interest, for proverbs are themselves part of the folk wisdom of a peasantry, understandable in its terms, whereas the depictions of peasants in the styles, themes, and genres of Flemish painting *creates* allegory by rendering the traditional subjects in analogic form; it humanizes them. Allegory came to be the form in which the meaning of Bruegel's pictures was imparted, and intended. Like the anthropologist, his invention of familiar ideas and themes in an exotic medium produced an automatic analogic extension of his world. And since these ideas and themes remained recognizable, their transformation in the process embodied the kind of resymbolization that we call allegory—analogy with a pointed significance.

The "bite" of Bruegel's particular kind of anthropology is most apparent in some of his street scenes depicting religious themes. These pictures recall the nearly contemporary dramas of Shakespeare in the universality of their vision, their concern to generalize human life by characterizing its immense variety. The resemblance is heightened by the fact that the humanism of both artists serves often as a means to interpret, comprehend, and even learn from the exotic. Shakespeare used the variety, brilliance, and wit of Elizabethan life as a seedbed of analogy for his penetration of ancient Rome, contemporary Venice, or medieval Denmark, and of course his depiction of their inhabitants as metaphorical Englishmen produced caricatures to delight his countrymen.

Likewise, the biblical villages portrayed in Bruegel's paintings *The Numbering at Bethlehem* and *The Massacre of the Innocents* are in every respect Flemish communities of the day. The occasions themselves, Mary and Joseph's arrival at Bethlehem for the census, or the soldiers of Herod intent on murdering the infant Jesus, can be recognized in the pictures; Mary has a blue cloak and is seated on a donkey, Joseph carries a carpenter's saw, a census is being taken, soldiers are harrying the populace, and so on. Otherwise, the village is snowbound in both scenes, the people are dressed as northern peasants, and the high, stepped rooves, the cropped trees, and the landscape itself are typical of the Low Countries. All these details served to "bring home" the events of the Bible, to make them believable and sympathetic to his audience, and, if pressed, Bruegel could have "explained" his efforts on that basis.

But the thrust of interpretation goes much deeper than mere "translation," for analogy always retains the potential of allegory. By showing figures and scenes from the Bible in a contemporary setting, Bruegel also implied the judgment of his own Flemish society in biblical terms. Thus the significance of *The Numbering at Bethlehem* is not only that "Jesus was born of man, in humble surroundings, just as people live today," but also that "if Mary and Joseph came to a Flemish town, they would *still* have to stay in a manger." *The Massacre of the Innocents* is even more pointed, for it depicts the soldiers of Herod, intent on murdering the Christ child, as the Spanish troops of the Habsburgs, ravaging the Low Countries for equally nefarious ends. Whether in art or anthropology, the elements we are forced to use as analogic "models" for the interpretation or explanation of our subject are themselves interpreted in the process.

We could go on to consider the development of Flemish painting from this point; Rubens' use of brushstroke to create an impressionistic art that played upon the viewer's expectations, or the superbly comprehensive works of masters like Rembrandt or Vermeer. As the tradition developed, its allegorical center of gravity changed, moving from the delineation on the canvas itself to the relation between artist (or viewer) and picture, and through this means to a highly sophisticated means of communication. As the meaningful content of painting came to be more and more clearly focused on the act of painting, symbolized in the emphasis on brushstroke, choice of subject, and so forth, the artists grew to realize a certain self-awareness. Rembrandt was an art collector, and Vermeer was a dealer as well, pursuits that were in both cases rendered appropriate by the intense personal (almost confessional) involvement that bound these men to every aspect of their work. So much of themselves was created through the realization of painting.

But we should return, at this point, and ask whether this degree of self-knowledge is attainable in our own discipline, whether a self-aware (rather than a self-conscious) anthropology is possible. Like the art of Rubens or Vermeer, such a science would be based on an intro- spective understanding of its own operations and capabilities; it would develop the relationship between technique and subject matter into a means of drawing self-knowledge from the understanding of others, and vice versa. Finally, it would make the selection and use of ex- planatory "models" and analogies from our own culture obvious and understandable as part of the simultaneous extension of our own understanding and penetration of other understandings. We would learn to externalize notions like "natural law," "logic," or even "cul- ture" (as Rembrandt did with his own demeanor and character in his self portraits), and, seeing them as we view the concepts of other peoples, come to apprehend our own meanings from a truly relative viewpoint.

The study of culture *is* culture, and an anthropology that wishes to be aware, and to develop its sense of relative objectivity, must come to terms with this fact. The study of culture is in fact *our* culture; it operates through our forms, creates in our terms, borrows our words and concepts for its meanings, and re-creates us through our efforts. And every anthropological undertaking therefore stands at a cross- roads: it can choose between an open-ended experience of mutual creativity, in which "culture" in general is created through the "cul- tures" that we use this concept to create, and a forcing of our own preconceptions onto other peoples. The crucial step—which is simul- taneously ethical and theoretical—is that of remaining true to the implications of our assumption of culture. If our culture is creative, then the "cultures" we study, as other examples of this phenomenon, must also be. For every time we make others part of a "reality" that we alone invent, denying their creativity by usurping the right to create, we *use* those people and their way of life and make them subservient to ourselves. And if creativity and invention emerge as *the* salient qualities of culture, then it is to these that our focus must now shift.

chapter 2

Culture as creativity

Fieldwork is work in the field

When I first went to do fieldwork among the Daribi people of New Guinea, I had certain expectations of what I hoped to accomplish, though of course I had few preconceived notions about what the people would be "like." Fieldwork is after all a kind of "work"; it is a creative, productive experience, although its "rewards" are not necessarily realized in the same way as are those of other forms of work. The fieldworker produces a kind of knowledge as a result of his experiences, a product that can be peddled as "qualifications" in the academic marketplace, or written into books. The resultant commodity falls into a class with other unique experiences: the memoirs of famous statesmen or entertainers, the journals of mountain climbers, arctic explorers, and adventurers, as well as accounts of exciting artistic or scientific achievements. Though they may attract special attention, such products are nonetheless products, and their creation is still "work."

The anthropologist in the field does work; his "working hours" are spent interviewing, observing and taking notes, taking part in local activities. I tried to structure my workday around a set pattern: breakfast followed by interviews with informants; then lunch, with perhaps some observational or participatory work, or perhaps more interviewing afterward; and then an evening meal. All sorts of things—visits, ceremonies, fights, as well as excursions—would interrupt the routine. Yet I clung to it, especially in the first few months, for the idea of regular, steady activity helped sustain my feeling of usefulness in the face of culture shock, the worries of "getting nowhere," and general frustrations. Even after many months, when I had come to understand the situation much better, and was more at ease with my Daribi friends, I still stuck to the rudiments of the schedule as a purposeful program for rounding out my knowledge of the culture.

I suspect that my tenacity in spite of the bemusement of my local friends (many of whom "worked" only in the morning on every other day) was simply the result of "wanting to do a good job," of a very Western idea of work and commitment to one's calling. Routines of this sort are not uncommon among anthropological fieldworkers—they form part of the general definition of the anthropologist's work (illusory though it may be): that we act upon the natives in such a way as to produce ethnographies. (Regardless of the subtleties of the fieldworker's involvement with the native culture, he initiates this involvement, and its results are regarded as his "production.") The totality of the ethnographer's interest in "culture" and the way he implements this interest in the field, then, is what defines his job as a fieldworker.

At first it was difficult for my Daribi friends to comprehend what this job—this interest in them and their ways—was, much less take it seriously. They would ask whether I was "government," "mission," or "doctor" (they were regularly visited by members of a leprosy control project), and being told that I was none of these, would marvel "he's not government, not mission, not a doctor!" When I discovered the pidgin term for anthropologist, *storimasta,* I used it as a label for my work, and the natives were able to "lump" me together with the linguistic missionaries they were familiar with. But, although it settled the matter of classification, this term did little to make my work believable to them. Why try and find out about other peoples' "stories," their ideas and ways of life? Who pays for this kind of work, and why? Is this a job for a grown man? (Query: Is our *storimasta* a grown man?)

If the work I did among the Daribi was problematic and puzzling, perhaps the way I lived would offer a clue to understanding it. As I was unmarried, my house was built next to the single men's residence, and since Daribi regard bachelorhood as an unenviable state, I received a good deal of commiseration and sympathy. A special point of interest was the fact that I had to hire a cook to prepare my meals; [1] his relationship to me became a matter of curiosity, and many came to investigate his duties and my household in general. Every night a small crowd of men and boys gathered to watch me eat my evening meal. The prevailing mood was one of curiosity and friendliness; although I tried to share my food, there was little enough even for me, and usually only three or four spectators managed to get a "taste." The mixture of wonder and companionship remained throughout my stay, though only gradually did I come to suspect its basis: the idea that my strange "work" was somehow related to my unmarried state.

No doubt the fact that I had to pay someone to cook for me was both strange and perhaps touching. The Daribi comment was often that "our wives are our cooks," and Daribi bachelors have to find food for themselves, or obtain it from their mothers or brothers' wives. Possibly I confirmed many suspicions when I answered questions about why I was not married by explaining that I preferred to finish my education and fieldwork first. My wifelessness continued to play on the sympathies of my neighbors, and when I persisted in pestering them for an account of how things came to be, it was a crucial factor in getting an answer. A middle-aged informant, who spent many of his odd hours bemoaning [2] his own unmarried state (he was actually responsible for the death of one of his wives), took pity on me, and revealed the local origin story "because you don't have a wife either, I'm sorry for you."

My status as representative white man made my situation even more intriguing to my Daribi friends. How did my peculiar interests relate to the specialties of other Europeans they knew of, such as the government, the missionaries, the doctors? Were these just names? Did they only stand for different kinds of work, or were they in fact separate and distinct families, or even different kinds of people? This was the sense of the question some of my friends put to me one afternoon: "Can you anthropologists intermarry with the government and the missionaries?" I explained that we could if we wanted to, but that I had no particular aspirations in that direction. But I had not answered

1. His most arduous jobs consisted of drawing water, washing dishes, and removing the small larvae that always managed to infest my brown rice supply.
2. He used the Daribi mourning lament, a drawn-out wailing.

the real question, so it was later rephrased and asked in a different way: "Are there *kanakas* (i.e., "natives, people like us") in America?" I said that there were, thinking of the subsistence farmers in some parts of the country, but I am afraid I conjured up an image of a subject population living under the tutelage of patrol officers, missionaries, and others.

The question was not one that could be posed easily in a few words, and so my answers, however "correct" they might be, were bound to mislead. And yet the problem was a vital one, for it turned upon the reasons for my presence in the village, and upon the nature of, and the motivation behind, the work I was doing. I was continually puzzled and sometimes annoyed by my friends' concern with what I took to be a side issue, the matter of my living arrangements and marital status, since I defined myself and justified my presence in terms of my anthropological interests and my fieldwork. The Daribi, for their part, were probably equally flabbergasted by my studied indifference to the problems of life and living, and my inexplicable passion for interviewing. (And after all, if I could ask them what kinds of people they were allowed to marry, it was only fair that they be able to ask me what kinds of people I could marry.)

The work that I had set out to do among the Daribi embodied a totally different notion of creativity, of what is important in life, from that which their own lives and work represented. My work was intended as creativity or production for its own sake, undertaken so as to add to the cumulative body of knowledge that we call "the anthropological literature." Its interests and motivations would necessarily be obscure and even misleading to someone who did not share our enthusiasm for this kind of production. Through this work I hoped to invent the Daribi people for my colleagues and countrymen, much as we have invented our own culture through the very same kind of creativity. But, given the circumstances, I could scarcely hope to portray Daribi creativity as a mirror image of our own.

For one thing, their attempts to "invent" me, to make me and my work believable, inevitably led to a kind of pity and commiseration which is the inverse of the maudlin compassion that philistines in our culture often profess for the benighted and unimproved "primitive." Their misunderstanding of me was not the same as my misunderstanding of them, and thus the difference between our respective interpretations could not be dismissed on the basis of linguistic dissimilarity or communicational difficulty. As my particular problem began with anthropology, and with my own (and our culture's) expectations of "culture" and creativity, let us turn once again to this subject as a key to the problem.

The ambiguity of "culture"

Our word "culture" derives in a very roundabout way from the past participle of the Latin verb *colere,* "to cultivate," and draws some of its meaning from this association with the tilling of the soil. This also seems to have been the major significance of the medieval French and English forms from which our present usage derives (for instance *cultura* meant "a plowed field" in Middle English). In later times "culture" took on a more specific sense, indicating a process of progressive refinement and breeding in the domestication of some particular crop, or even the result or increment of such a process. Thus we speak of agriculture, apiculture, the "culture of the vine," or of a bacterial culture.

The contemporary "opera-house" sense of the word arises from an elaborate metaphor, which draws upon the terminology of crop breeding and improvement to create an image of man's control, refinement, and "domestication" of himself. So, in the drawing rooms of the eighteenth and nineteenth centuries, one spoke of a "cultivated" person as someone who "had culture," who had developed his interests and accomplishments along approved lines, training and "breeding" the personality as a natural strain might be "cultured."

The anthropological usage of "culture" constitutes a further metaphorization, if not a democratization, of this essentially elitist and aristocratic sense. It amounts to an abstract extension of the notion of human refinement and domestication from the individual to the collective, so that we can speak of culture as man's general control, refinement, and improvement of himself, rather than one man's conspicuousness in this respect. Applied in this way, the word also carries strong connotations of Locke's and Rousseau's conception of the "social contract," of the tempering of man's "natural" instincts and desires by an arbitrary imposition of will. The nineteenth-century concept of "evolution" added a historical dimension to this notion of man's breeding and tempering of himself, resulting in the optimistic concept of "progress."

Regardless of its more specific associations, however, our modern term "culture" retains the several associations, and hence the creative ambiguity, introduced by these metaphorizations. The confusion of "culture" in the "opera-house" sense with the more general anthropological sense actually amounts to a continuous derivation of one significance from the other.[3] It is in the area of this ambiguity, with

3. The earlier "derivation" of the opera-house sense of the word from the agricultural probably also coincided with a similar confusion and creative ambiguity.

its contrasting implications, that we might expect to find a clue to what we most often intend in our use of the word.

When we speak of the "cultural centers," or even the "culture" of the city of Chicago, we mean a certain kind of institution. We do not mean steel mills, airports, grocery stores, or service stations, although these would be included in the more catholic anthropological definitions. The "cultural institutions" of a city are its museums, libraries, symphony orchestras, universities, and perhaps its parks and zoos. It is in these specialized sanctuaries, set apart from everyday life by special regulations, endowed by special funds, and guarded by highly qualified personnel, that the documents, records, relics, and embodiments of man's greatest achievements are kept, and "art" or "culture" is kept alive. The idea of a musical "conservatory" is a case in point, for it provides a reverent atmosphere within which the study, practice, recitals, and concerts necessary to the "life" of music can be carried on. Cultural institutions not only preserve and protect the results of man's refinement, they also sustain it and provide for its continuation.

The connection between this "institutional" Culture and the more universal concept of the anthropologist is not immediately apparent, though it is in fact only thinly disguised by the facades of libraries, museums, and opera houses. For the very core of our own culture, in the accepted image, is its science, art, and technology, the sum total of achievements, inventions, and discoveries that define our idea of "civilization." These achievements are preserved (in institutions), taught (in other institutions), and added to (in research institutions) in a cumulative process of refinement. We preserve a vast panoply of ideas, facts, relics, secrets, techniques, applications, formulas, and documents as our "culture," the sum of our ways of doing things, and the sum of "knowledge" as we know it. This "culture" exists in a broad and a narrow, an "unmarked" and a "marked" sense.

The productiveness or creativity of our culture is defined by the application, manipulation, reenactment, or extension of these techniques and discoveries. Work of any kind, whether innovative or simply what we call "productive," achieves its meaning in relation to this cultural sum, which forms its meaningful context. When a plumber replaces a pipe he draws upon a complex of interlinked technological discoveries and productive efforts. His act becomes significant as "work" through its integration into this complex; it applies and carries forth certain technological inventions (as a "Cultural institution" might), and both defines the plumber as a worker and relates his efforts in a complementary way to those of other workers. The work of the anthropologist also does this; it draws upon a pool of skills and insights that can be acquired by "education," and contributes to a totality called "the anthropological literature."

Meaningful, productive work, which is also called "labor," is the basis of our credit system, and we can therefore assess it in monetary terms. This makes it possible to evaluate other quantities, such as time, resources, and accumulated labor, or even abstract "rights" and "obligations." This productivity, the application and implementation of man's refinement of himself, provides the central focus of our civilization. This explains the high valuation placed upon "Culture" in the narrow, marked, opera-house sense, for it represents the creative increment, the productivity that creates work and knowledge by providing its ideas, techniques, and discoveries, and that ultimately shapes cultural value itself. We experience the relation between the two senses of "culture" in the meanings of our everyday life and work: "Culture" in the more restricted sense stands as a historical and normative precedent for culture as a whole; it embodies an ideal of human refinement.

It is because work and productivity are central to our system of values that we base our credit system on them. "Money," or "wealth," is therefore the symbol of work, of the production of things and services according to techniques that are the preserved heritage of our historical development. Although some of these techniques are patented, some formulas secret, and some skills the property of particular people, the larger part of our technology and cultural heritage is public knowledge, made available through public education. As money represents the public standard of exchange, so education defines a certain prerequisite for participation.

And yet if productivity is public, the family can be said to be peripheral and private. Money, and therefore work, is necessary to "support" a family, but neither money nor labor should be the primary consideration within the family. Regardless of how it is earned or budgeted, the family income is *shared* to some degree among the members, but it is not apportioned in exchange for family services. As Schneider's *American Kinship* has shown, relations within the family are symbolized in terms of love, sexual love, or a relationship of "enduring, diffuse solidarity." The opposition between money and love dramatizes the sharp separation drawn in our culture between "business" and "home life."

Love is traditionally the thing that "money cannot buy," and duty is supposed to be above personal considerations. Thus the stories about liaisons between businessmen and their secretaries, doctors and their nurses, or pilots and their stewardesses are celebrated scandals, as are accounts of film or television stars who marry for the sake of their images. And of course the role of the prostitute, who does "for money" what other women do "for love," and who lives in "a house that is not a home," symbolizes an antiworld of vice and corruption for many Americans. Interpersonal relations, and especially family relations, should be private and "above" monetary interests; one should not "use" them for financial gain.

Apart from the speculations of some anthropologists, family life and interpersonal relations play an almost negligible part in the historical accounts that are generally used to validate our cultural self-image. Typically, these myths are obsessed with man's development as a history of productive techniques, a gradual accumulation of "tools" and "adaptations" indicating progressively greater technological sophistication. It is not difficult to recall the lists of great advances taught in high school: fire, attributed to "prehistoric" man, the alphabet, the wheel, the Roman arch, the Franklin stove, and so on. Regardless of the dates, the names, or the specific inventions, "Culture" emerges as an accumulation, a sum of great inventions and mighty achievements. It amounts, in fact, to a tightly controlled linking of the broad, abstract notion of "culture" to the more narrow sense of the word, minimizing ambiguity.

The thought that there are parts of the world where wives can be purchased has often presented a kind of imaginative fool's paradise for those who could bring themselves to believe that the control of women could ever be so simple. But in the light of our discussion of money and love in our own culture, the yearnings must necessarily be dismissed as a form of prostitution fantasy. Moreover, the assumption that wives are "bought" and "sold" in tribal societies involves the most profound misunderstanding of these peoples. In the words of Francis Bugotu, a native of the Solomon Islands:

> The buying of wives in primitive societies has no equivalence with the pecuniary exchanges of the West. Money is not important and certainly not the attraction. It is the woman who is valuable.[4]

What we would call "production" in these societies belongs to the symbolization of even the most intimate personal relationships. For the Melanesian, "work" can be anything from weeding a garden to

---

4. F. Bugotu, "The Culture Clash," *New Guinea and Australia, the Pacific and Southeast Asia*, 3:2 (June/July, 1968), 67.

taking part in a feast or begetting a child; its validation comes from the part it plays in human interaction. The work of "making a living" takes place within a family, whose members assume complementary roles corresponding to the cultural image of their sex and age group. Thus "production" is what men and women, or men, women, and children do together; it defines them socially in their several roles, and also symbolizes the meaning of the family. A man is limited to certain capabilities, perhaps, as among the Daribi, to the felling of trees, fencing of gardens, and tending of certain crops. Other tasks fall to the women, and a man would not attempt them without shame, or even worse damage to his self-image. A kind of intersexual integration, which we call by analogy "marriage" is as necessary for subsistence as it is for the creation of children, so that sexual relations and productivity are part of the same totality, which we might call "the production of people."

Since the family *is* "production" in this kind of society, it is self-sustaining, and there is no need to "support" it. But a system of this kind makes "marriage" and the family a matter of life and death; a person who does not marry cannot produce, and is doomed to a servile dependence on others. Thus the central problem of the young man, celebrated in myth and proverb, becomes that of finding a wife. Whereas products themselves, or money with which to buy products, are not in demand, *producers* are; since all major aspects of sustenance are vested in the family, the paramount concern becomes that of forming and sustaining a family. So it is that the exchange systems of tribal and peasant societies are geared to the human life cycle and the substitution of "wealth" for persons. People are indispensable, and therefore the most valuable things known are pressed into service to control their distribution. It is the details of this substitution, the control, exchange, and distribution of people, that anthropologists have understood as "social structure."

Because it is a part of interpersonal relations, and an embodiment of human, rather than abstract values, the productivity of tribal societies is not obsessed with tools or techniques. The basic techniques of production, clearing land, building houses, weaving, or processing food, are incorporated within sexual roles, and are part of being male or female. More specialized techniques, or the concern with skill and technique in themselves, are peripheral and individual. Anthropologists know these pursuits as "magic," "sorcery," and "shamanism," the development and hoarding of often secret techniques to ensure personal success.

Thus tribal cultures embody an inversion of our tendency to place productive technique in the central focus, and relegate family life to a supporting (and supported) role. This inversion, moreover, is not trivial; it pervades both styles of creativity in all of their aspects. As we produce "things," so our concern is with preserving things, products, and the techniques of their production. Our Culture is a sum of such things: we keep the ideas, the quotations, the memoirs, the creations, and let the people go. Our attics, basements, trunks, albums, and museums are full of this kind of Culture.

On the other hand, the suggestion that tribal peoples are "materialists," one that is often applied in the case of the New Guinea highlanders, makes as little sense as the accusation that they "buy" wives. Here, as Bugotu says, it is the people who are important; wealth consists of "counters" for people, and, far from being hoarded, it is dispersed often at death through death payments. It is people, and the experiences and meanings associated with them, that they do not want to lose, rather than ideas and things. My New Guinean friends transfer the names of the newly dead to the newly born, and also find it necessary to invent the deceased in the form of ghosts, so that they are not wholly lost. We do much the same kind of thing with books, which are our "ghosts," our past, wherein so much of what we call our "Culture" lives.

Because these are styles of creativity that we have been discussing, and not merely "types of society," they characterize human invention in a total and comprehensive way. And because the perception and comprehension of others can only proceed by a kind of analogy, knowing them through an extension of the familiar, each style of creativity is also a style of understanding. The New Guineans see the anthropologist's creativity as *being* his interaction with them, rather than resulting from it. They perceive the fieldworker to be "doing" life, rather as Zorba the Greek might see him, a bold and inclusive sort of "life." And, as in all such cases, one wants to help the foolhardy foreigner. Or at least pity him.

For his part, the anthropologist assumes that the native is doing what *he* is doing, namely "culture." And so, as a way of understanding his subject, the fieldworker is obliged to invent a culture for him, as a plausible thing to be doing. But since plausibility is a function of the researcher's viewpoint, the "culture" that he imagines for the native is bound to bear a distinct relation to that which he claims for himself.

When an anthropologist studies another culture, he "invents" it by generalizing his impressions, experiences, and other evidences as if they were produced by some external "thing." Thus his invention is an objectification, or reification, of that "thing." But if the culture he invents is to have meaning for his fellow anthropologists, as well as other compatriots, there must be a further control on his invention. It must be believable and meaningful in terms of his own image of "culture." We have seen that the term "culture" has no one referent for us: its successive and several meanings are created by a series of metaphorizations, "ambiguities," if you prefer. When we identify some set of observations or experiences as a "culture," we extend our idea of culture to encompass new details, and increase its possibilities as well as its ambiguity. In an important way, the hypothetical "invention" of a culture by an anthropologist constitutes an act of extension; it is a new and unique "derivation" of the abstract sense of "culture" from the more narrow sense.

But if the abstract, anthropological notion of "culture" depends on the "opera-house" notion for its meaning, the reverse is also true. Nor is the issue limited to these two variants; newer constructs like "subculture" or "counterculture" metaphorize the anthropological term to create an even greater richness, and also a shift, of meaning. The semantic possibilities of the concept "culture" remain a function of this richness and this interplay of allusion and innuendo. Anthropological writing has tended to conserve the ambiguity of culture, for this ambiguity is continually enhanced by the identification of provocatively new and different "cultures," and continually controlled through the formation of explanatory analogies.

It is not surprising, then, that anthropologists should be so fascinated with tribal peoples, with modes of thought whose lack of anything like our notion of "culture" teases our generalizations into fantastic shapes and extremes. These subjects are provocative and interesting for that very reason, because they introduce the "play" of greater possibilities and more extensive generalization into the concept of "culture." Nor should we be surprised if the resultant analogies and "models" seem awkward and ill-fitting, for they are born of the paradox created by imagining a culture for people who do not imagine it for themselves. These constructs are tentative bridges to meaning, they are part of our understanding, not its object, and we treat them as "real" at the peril of turning anthropology into a wax museum of curiosities, reconstructed fossils, and great moments from imaginary histories.

The wax museum

It is perhaps no accident that much of the earliest anthropology developed in museums, and that museums are Cultural institutions in the "marked" sense of the word. For museums form the logical point of transition or articulation between the two major senses of "culture";

they metaphorize ethnographic specimens and data by analyzing and preserving them, making them necessary to our own refinement although they belong to some other culture. The totem poles, Egyptian mummies, arrowheads, and other relics in our museums are "culture" in two senses: they are simultaneously products of their makers and of anthropology, which is "cultural" in the narrow sense. Because these medicine bundles, pots, blankets, and other items were elemental to the museum's definition and reconstruction of their "cultures," they came to have the same significance as the strategic relics that *we* seek to preserve: the first sewing machine, revolutionary war muskets, or Benjamin Franklin's spectacles. The study of "primitives" had become a function of our invention of the past.

In this light it is scarcely astonishing that Ishi, the last surviving Yahi Indian in California, spent the years after his surrender living in a museum.[5] Museums had by then assumed fully the role of a reservation for Indian culture, and we are told that in good weather Kroeber and others would take Ishi back into the hills so that he could demonstrate Yahi techniques and bushcraft. In spite of Kroeber's deep sympathy for Ishi, one cannot help feeling that he was the ideal museum specimen, one that did the anthropologist's job for him by producing and reconstituting its own culture. This suggestion makes it easy to forget that Ishi's job as an Indian was primarily that of living, and that he had merely exchanged his fugitive existence for a formaldehyde sinecure. But this, again, is precisely the point; by accepting employment as a museum specimen, Ishi accomplished the metaphorization of life into culture that defines much of anthropological understanding.

If Ishi brought the world into the museums, then Tylor's earlier doctrine of "survivals" had brought the museum into the world. For if the "nonproductive" aspects of cultural life, like Morgan's idea of kinship, can be understood as surviving traits of an earlier evolutionary stage, then like the "nonproductive" Indian, they were fossils. The early evolutionists were willing to accept productive life as self-evidently meaningful, and to reserve the remainder for their own productive invention of the past. But the reflexive sense of this metaphorization made the whole world of "custom" into a gigantic living museum, which only anthropologists were privileged to interpret. It was not simply the museum, but man's life itself, that constantly recreated the past.

5. Theodora Kroeber, *Ishi in Two Worlds* (Berkeley and Los Angeles: University of California Press, 1963).

In both Tylor's and Ishi's cases, "culture" in the abstract, anthropological sense was a reified artifact of "Culture" in the narrow, marked sense. Because this invention, or derivation, took place in the context of museums and of our historical self-identification, the resultant notion of culture assumed the characteristics of a museum assemblage. It was finite, discrete, and unequivocal; it had peculiar "styles" and "usages" that could be determined with great precision. One might not be able to tell whether a given Indian was *really* Cheyenne or Arapaho, even by questioning him closely, but there was never any doubt about styles and artifacts. Beneath the sheltering aegis of our "Cultural institutions" a series of distinct "cultures" and a general conception of culture were developed, which were in every way analogous to our "marked" sense of Culture as an accumulation of great ideas, inventions, and achievements.

In many respects this idea of culture has never left the anthropological imagination. Our attempts to metaphorize tribal peoples as "Culture" have reduced them to technique and artifact; our attempts to produce these cultures ethnologically, to comprehend the "artifact" by reproducing it, result in overdetermined "systems." The logic of a society where "culture" is a conscious and deliberate thing, where life subserves some purpose, rather than the reverse, and where every fact or proposition is required to have a reason, creates a strangely surrealistic effect when applied to tribal peoples. So little, in fact, are these "functions," "social facts," or "logical structures of the mind" believable in one's experiences with natives as people "on the ground," that we are forced into the position that the "reasons" and "purposes" adduced theoretically are subliminal, subconscious, or implicit universal properties.

The result has been an overburdening of the generalized concept of culture, cramming it full of explanatory logics, levels, and heuristic enforcement systems until it appears as the very metaphor of "order." Such a "culture" is totally predicated, it is rule, grammar and lexicon, or necessity, a complete perfusing of rigid form and paradigm throughout the range of human thought and action; in Freudian terms, it approximates a collective compulsion. Moreover, since this ironclad "order" simultaneously represents our means of comprehending the culture, change or variation can only be approached negatively, as a kind of entropy, static, or "noise."

In the search for analogues to our logical, legal, political, and economic orders among tribal peoples we have seized upon all manner of conventional, symbolic, and idiomatic usage for transformation into "structure." This is particularly evident in social anthropology, where the meanings attached to interpersonal relationships are often literalized in terms of their symbolic components: kinship is reduced to biology, or to genealogical paradigms, and society itself is truncated into a set of mechanisms for the shuffling about of people and goods. Here again we are brought face to face with Francis Bugotu's dictum: it is the people that are important, not the economics and mechanics of their transfer. An approach that sees the African marriage-cattle, virtually a matrix of social metaphor, as economic "property," or one that interprets the Australian aborigine marriage systems as clever computer programming, or dizzy permutations of the incest taboo, has effectively vivisected the native meanings in the attempt to understand them.

The study of such exotic modes of conceptualization actually amounts to a resymbolization of them, transforming their symbols into ours, which is why they so often appear in reduced or literalized form. An anthropology that refuses to accept the universality of mediation, that reduces meaning to belief, dogma, and certainty, is forced into the trap of having to believe either the native meanings or our own. The former alternative, we are told, is superstitious and unobjective; the latter, according to some, is "science." And yet this kind of science can easily degenerate into a form of indirect speech, a way of making provocative points by translating idiom into fact and by overexoticizing one's research subjects for symbolic effect. This is possible because anthropology is always necessarily mediative, whether it is aware of the implications or not; culture, as the mediative term, is a way of describing others as we would describe ourselves, and vice versa.

A true metaphorization of the diverse phenomena of human life and thought in terms of our notion of "culture" would necessarily have to carry across the creative invention that we manifest in the act of studying another people. Otherwise we are forced into the explicitly false posture of creating ambiguities within our own concepts so as to prove the precise, strictly determined, and unambiguous nature of other peoples' concepts, of inventing systems that cannot invent and calling them "culture." As long as the anthropological concept remains even partially dependent upon the opera house sense of the term, our studies of other peoples, and particularly of tribal societies, will be skewed in the direction of our own self-image.

Anthropology will not come to terms with its mediative basis and its professed aims until our invention of other cultures can reproduce, at least in principle, the way in which those cultures invent themselves. We must be able to experience our subject matter directly, as alternative meaning, rather than indirectly, through literalization or reduction to the terms of our ideologies. The issue can be phrased in practical, philosophical, or ethical language, but in any case it devolves upon the question of what we *want* to mean by the word "culture," and how we choose to resolve, and to invent, its ambiguities.

"Road belong culture"

If "culture" becomes paradoxical and challenging when applied to the meanings of tribal societies, we might speculate as to whether a "reverse anthropology" is possible, literalizing the metaphors of modern industrial civilization from the standpoint of tribal society. Surely we have no right to expect a parallel theoretical effort, for the ideological concern of these people puts them under no obligation to specialize in this way, or to propound philosophies for the lecture room. In other words, our "reverse anthropology" will have nothing to do with "culture," with production for its own sake, though it might have a great deal to do with the quality of life. And if human beings are as generally inventive as we have assumed, it would be very surprising if such a "reverse anthropology" did not already exist.

It does, of course. As a result of the political and economic expansion of European society in the nineteenth century, many of the world's tribal peoples found themselves in a "fieldwork" situation through no fault of their own. "Fieldwork" is perhaps a euphemism for what was often little more than a sustained, cumulative culture shock, and yet there is a parallel, for culture shock forces one to objectify, to seek comprehension. We call these attempts at comprehension many things, for they assume many forms, and yet the most familiar terms betray the activist form that concerted thought must assume among peoples where thought is a part of life: cargo cult and millenarian movement.

If we call such phenomena "cargo cults," then anthropology should perhaps be called a "culture cult," for the Melanesian "kago" is very much the interpretive counterpart of our word "culture." The words are to some extent "mirror images" of each other, in the sense that we look at the natives' cargo, their techniques and artifacts, and call it "culture," whereas they look at our culture and call it "cargo." These are analogic usages, and they betray as much about the interpreters themselves as about the thing interpreted. "Cargo" is practically a parody, a reduction of Western notions like profit, wage-labor, and production for its own sake to the terms of tribal society. It is, paradoxically, no more materialistic than the Melanesian marriage practices, and this is the key to its apocalyptic and millenarian associations

The "cargo" is seldom thought of in the way we might expect, as simple material wealth; its significance is based rather on the symbolic use of European wealth to represent the redemption of native society. In this usage it resembles those other "cargoes," the more traditionally symbolic constituents of the bride price, or the activity and products of gardening, that embody the central meaning of human relations for Melanesians, and that *we* tend to interpret in materialist, economic terms. Cargo is really an antisymbol to "culture"; it metaphorizes the sterile orders of technique and self-fulfilling production as life and human relation, just as "culture" does the reverse. In the words of Kenelm Burridge, who distinguishes a capitalized sense of "cargo" from the ordinary sense, much as we have done with "culture":

> It is clear that if cargo means manufactured goods, Cargo embraces a set of acute moral problems; that Cargo movements are not due simply to a misunderstanding concerning the origin of manufactured goods, but that they are embodied in, and arise from, a complex total situation. . . .[6]

The symbol of "cargo," quite as much as that of "culture," draws its force and its meaning from its ambiguities; it is simultaneously the enigmatic and tantalizing phenomenon of Western material goods and their profound human implication for the native mind. When the symbol is invoked, the second of these senses incorporates the first into a powerful analogous relation, which both restructures the phenomenon and gives it meaning. This relation, and the meaning that it compels, encompasses all aspects of the moral dilemma; it is access to the cargo, the rapport entailed by a sharing of the cargo, and the millennial conditions necessary for the arrival of the cargo. Moreover, since "cargo," like "culture," is a term of mediation between different peoples, the relation that it embodies becomes that of Melanesian to Western society.

The fact that "cargo" and "culture" metaphorize the same inter-societal relation, while doing so in opposite directions, so to speak, makes them effectively metaphorizations of each other. "Culture" extends the significance of technique, mode, and artifact to human thought and relationship; "cargo" extends that of human relation and mutual production to manufactured artifacts: each concept uses the extensive bias of the other as its symbol. Thus it is easy for Westerners to "literalize" the significance of "cargo," and assume that it means simply manufactured goods, or Western modes of production, "Culture," that is, in the narrow sense. This kind of simplification, the

---

6. Kenelm Burridge, *Mambu: A Study of Melanesian Cargo Movements and Their Ideological Background* (New York and Evanston: Harper & Row, 1970), p. 246.

short-circuiting of a symbol, is in fact the popularized, Sunday-supple-
ment view of cargo cult, a counterpart of mission ideology about saving
the "lost" heathens, or the sentimentality that perceives tribal peoples
as impoverished relatives begging for a transistorized handout.

But it is also shown most graphically in Peter Lawrence's analysis
of the career of Yali, the cult leader from the north coast of New
Guinea, that the reverse is true; that Melanesians, when they encounter the notion of "culture," have a tendency to interpret it as
"cargo" in their sense. When Yali, whose cooperation was being so-
licited by the Australian Administration, was taken to Port Moresby
in 1947, he was astounded by two things. The first of these was a shift
in administration policy favoring and even encouraging native custom
and ceremonial; the second was his discovery that not all Europeans
subscribe to the mission religions and the Adam and Eve story.[7] He
was intrigued by diagrams illustrating the course of evolution, and
especially by the *monki,* and rather perceptively linked this theory to
the Western practice of keeping animals in zoos. Lawrence argues
cogently that Yali regarded this emphasis on natural history as a
kind of totemism,[8] a shrine, as it were, for the preservation of social
relations.

The point is made more concisely by Yali's later interpretation of
some New Guinean artifacts he had seen in a Queensland museum
during the Second World War. According to Lawrence, "Yali himself
had described the artifacts in these terms: 'Our myths are there
also' . . . The word 'myth' *(perambik, sitori)* in this context broadly
connoted 'New Guinea culture.'" [9] Yali's experiences with the way
Westerners think about and preserve their past, and tolerate and preserve the pasts of others, gave him a greater realization of "culture"
than most Melanesians are able to acquire. Invariably, however, this
notion of culture was assimilated to, and mistaken for his own "cargo"
expectations. The "road belong cargo" became the "road belong culture," as is evident in the upshot of Yali's Port Moresby episode, for
he returned to his native Madang area to initiate a full-scale revival
of traditional ceremonies in order to bring the cargo.

Yali's revival was by no means an attempted replication of pre-
colonial life; it was characterized by a frenetic overindulgence in
ceremonial, as well as the incorporation of practices from earlier cults.

7. Peter Lawrence, *Road Belong Cargo: A Study of the Cargo Movement in the
Southern Madang District, New Guinea* (Manchester: Manchester University Press,
1964), pp. 173–78.

8. Ibid., pp. 174–75.

9. Ibid., p. 191.

Like similar "revivals" elsewhere in the world, this one was not concerned with "culture" itself, but with culture as a symbol of something else. Although identity is involved, as it must always be when "culture" is assumed self-consciously, identity by no means exhausts or explains the usage, for culture always figures in such revivals as an access to things far more important than culture could ever be.

People like Yali, it is said, are driven to these interpretive extremes by social injustice, exploitation, and the stresses of something called "culture-contact." Certainly the peoples of the Madang littoral had had their fill of exploitation and humiliation by successive waves of German, Australian, and Japanese colonialists; bizarre religious sectarians had hoped to win an audience among allegedly "simple" tribesmen for ideas that their countrymen had come to regard as all too simple. Yet I do not propose to account for Yali's motivation and creativity in this way, if only because explanations in terms of disturbance and injustice belittle human achievements to the level of correctives, and reduce life to an equilibrium model. It says little enough of that leader of the first Jesus movement, Joshua of Nazareth, to trace his ideas and purpose to Roman injustice, or the difference in living standard between Romans and Palestinians.

Moreover, our discussion has shown that there is no reason to treat cargo cult as anything but an interpretive counterpart of anthropology itself, and that its creativity need not be any more problematic than that of the anthropologists who study it. Cargo cult can be thought of as a pragmatic sort of anthropology that invents in anticipation of the future, in a manner reminiscent of Melanesian magic, rather than reconstructing the past or present out of shards of evidence. It is clear from the foregoing that devotees of either concept, cargo or culture, cannot easily apprehend the other without turning it into their own, yet it is also clear that this characteristic is not limited to cultists or anthropologists alone, that all men project, tease, and extend their ideas as analogies into a world of intransigent phenomena.

It is elemental to a definition of man that he continually invests his ideas, seeking external equivalents that not only articulate them, but also subtly change them in the process, until often these meanings take on a life of their own, and possess their authors. Man is the shaman of his meanings. The ambiguity of culture, and that of cargo, coincides with the power such a concept has in the hands of its interpreters, who use the points of analogy to manage and control the paradoxical aspects. Yet these selfsame interpreters, like all shamans, are also subject to the vagaries of their familiars, which goes some way toward explaining the incongruities of Yali and his anthropological counterparts.

chapter 3

The power of invention

Invention is culture

We have seen in the preceding chapters that anthropology is the study of man through the assumption of culture, a notion that includes the thoughts and actions of both the anthropologist and his subjects as varieties of the same phenomenon. In its broadest and simplest connotation, "culture" provides a relativistic basis for the understanding of other peoples. We study culture through culture, and so whatever operations characterize our investigation must also be general properties of culture. If invention is indeed the most crucial aspect of our understanding of other cultures, then this must be of central significance in the way in which all cultures operate. If, in other words, we admit to the anthropologist's creativity in building his comprehension of a culture, we can scarcely deny the same sort of creativity to the culture itself and its members.

Invention, then, *is* culture, and it might be helpful to think of all human beings, wherever they may be, as "fieldworkers" of a sort, controlling the culture shock of daily experience through all kinds of imagined and constructed "rules," traditions, and facts. The anthropologist makes his experiences understandable (to himself as well as to others in his society) by perceiving them and understanding them in terms of his own familiar way of life, his Culture. He invents them as "culture." And because he has learned all his life to communicate with others, his friends and family as well as his colleagues, through the shared conventions of this Culture, he is now able to communicate with members of a different society through the "culture" he has invented for them. Because his subject culture has become meaningful to him in the way that his own life is meaningful, he is able to communicate his experiences of it to those who share the meanings and conventions of his own way of life.

If we assume that every human being is an "anthropologist," an inventor of culture, then it follows that all people need a set of shared conventions similar in some way to our collective "Culture" in order to communicate and understand their experiences. And if invention is truly as basic to human existence as I have suggested, then communication and the set of shared conventions and associations that allow communication to take place are equally basic. All meaningful expression, and therefore all experience and understanding, is a kind of invention, and invention requires a communicational base in shared conventions if it is to be meaningful—that is if it is to allow us to relate what we do, say, and feel to others, and to the world of meanings that we share with them. Expression and communication are interdependent: neither is possible without the other.

Our discussion of cargo cult and of production in tribal society has shown how inadequate the Western Culture of collective enterprise is as a model for the self-invention of tribal peoples. If the communicational basis of Yali's invention is so different from our own, an understanding of culture as invention requires that we consider the whole matter of communication and inventive expression in some detail. What do we mean by the "conventional associations" of a word or some other symbolic element, how do they objectify "reality"; and what is the relation of their "conventionalness" to the kind of extension that I have equated with invention? How, in other words, is invention related to man's larger conception of himself and the world? I will try to answer this question generally at first, and then through the use of specific examples taken from modern American culture. But its implications are at once so crucial and so general that they encompass our conceptions of "self" and of motivation as well as society and the surrounding world. Thus if we wish to take invention seriously we must be prepared to forego many of our assumptions about what is "real" and why people act as they do.

Words like "invention" and "innovation" are often used to distinguish novel acts or ideas, or things created for the first time, from actions, thoughts, and arrangements that have become established, or habitual. Such a distinction conceals an assumption of the "automatic" or "determined" nature of ordinary action quite as much as deterministic notions do. By extending the usage of "invention" and "innovation" to the whole range of thought and action, I mean to counteract this assumption and to assert the spontaneous and creative realization of human culture.

Communication and meaningful expression are carried on through the use of symbolic elements, words, images, gestures, or sequences of these. When isolated and viewed as "things" in themselves, these elements seem to be merely arbitrary noises, patterns of light, or motions. (As an example, try repeating a word like "zeppelin" or "poppy" over and over again, concentrating on the sound alone, and see how peculiar it sounds after awhile.) These elements are meaningful to us only through their *associations,* which they acquire through being associated with or opposed to one another in all sorts of *contexts.* Meaning is therefore a function of the ways in which we create and otherwise experience contexts.

The word "context" has been used extensively by modern linguists in search of a relational basis or matrix for meaningful word-use. It generally connotes the meaningful "environment" in which a symbol is used. But it eludes precise bounding and definition to a degree that exasperates linguists—my colleague Oswald Werner calls it the "snake oil" of linguistic explanation. I have used the term in the broadest possible way, applying it to any bunch of symbolic elements that in any sense occur together, whether they form a recognizable sequence or entity (the "syntagmatic chain" of some writers), or enter into opposition as contrasting aspects of a distinction (the basis of a "paradigmatic" relation). I have chosen to generalize "context" with the anticipation that a concept that defies constructive *narrowing* might serve us better by being *broadened*—after the manner of the mathematical concept of "set" in "set theory."

A context is a part of experience—and also something that our experience constructs; it is an environment within which symbolic elements relate to one another; one that is formed by the act of relating them. The elements in a conventionally recognized context seem to *belong* together, as elephants, tents, clowns, and acrobats "belong" to a circus. Some elements are less conventionally a part of such a context than others, though this varies from time to time and from place to place. For example, a dancing bear is less conventionally a part of a circus for Americans than it is for Europeans. Some contexts are less conventional than others, though this too varies with time, place, and people. The more conventional ones may be so familiar that they are perceived as wholes, things, or experiences in their own right, like "wintertime," "school," or the Declaration of Independence. Others are more obviously "put together," like the bunch of words that make up an unfamiliar poem, or a schedule that one has not yet learned to live with.

There are no perceptible limits to the amount or the extent of the contexts that can exist in a given culture. Some contexts include others, and make them a part of their articulation; others may be interrelated in ways that do not involve total inclusion or exclusion. Some seem so traditional as to be almost permanent and unchanging, and yet new ones are created all the time in the production of statements and situations that is everyday life.

Any given symbolic element can be involved in many cultural contexts, and the articulation of these contexts can vary from one moment to the next, from one person to another, or from one group of people to another. Yet communication and expression are possible only to the extent that the parties involved share and understand these contexts and their articulations. If the contextual associations of a symbolic element are shared, then the significance of their extension or "borrowing" for use in another context will also be shared.

A word or some other symbolic element receives its conventional associations from the part it plays in the articulations of the contexts in which it occurs, and from the relative importance and significance of those contexts. When an element is invoked outside of such a context, we draw upon and make use of the character, reality, and importance of the context as "associations" of the element. In this regard a word or other element can be said to relate all of the contexts in which it appears, and to relate these, directly or indirectly, through any novel usage or "extension."

Our word "father" carries the associations of biological kinship (as in a paternity suit), kin relationships (acting like a father), religious cosmology ("Our Father, which art in heaven . . ."), and religious office ("the Jesuit Fathers"), among many others. It relates these, directly and indirectly, in many specific ways, some of which compel meanings that are as important in their own right as the transformation of opera-house Culture into anthropological culture that we explored in the previous chapter. "Father" has a broad range of "conventional" meanings and associations, a specific ("narrow") association with each of its conventional contexts, an incalculable spread of "personal" or idiosyncratic associations for different individuals, groups, and periods, and a virtually infinite potential for the creation of new meanings through all of these.

Any time we use such a word in some specific context we "extend" its other contextual associations. *We can only define a symbolic element, or assign priorities to its various conventional associations, on the basis of the (assumed) relative significance of the contexts in which it participates.* Thus definition comes to be an exercise in asserting or adjusting the definer's cultural viewpoint, his priorities and conventions of communication. If we judge biological kinship to be more "basic" than religious cosmology, then the primary associations of "father" are natural and biological, and the use of this word in reference to the Godhead is an "extension." Apart from this kind of ideological commitment, there are no "primary" meanings, and *the definition and the extension of a word or other symbolic element are fundamentally the same operation.* Every use of a symbolic element is an innovative extension of the associations it acquires through its conventional integration into other contexts.

Meaning is thus a product of relation, and the meaningful properties of a definition are no less results of relating than those of any other expressive construct. And yet meaning would always be completely relative if it were not for the mediation of convention—the illusion that some associations of a symbolic element are "primary" and self-evident. If meaning is based on relation, then the good, solid feeling of "absolute" denotation (upon which so many linguistic epistemologies are founded) is an illusion grounded in nonrelation, or tautology. It corresponds to the effect of a context that "gives itself associations" through its own articulating elements. When we use "father" in a family context, it carries associations of biological paternity, and perhaps divinity, but it also carries forth the very "familial" associations that link this particular application with other instances of the same sort. Calling one's father a "father" gives the familial context its own associations back. It gives the good, comfortable (and somewhat trite) sense of using a word in the way that it ought to be used, and this usage appears self-evident. The more completely this effect of "giving itself characteristics" is realized, the more *conventionalized*, widely shared, communicable, easily defined (and meaningless) the usage can be said to be. Or, to put it differently, the things we can define best are the things least worth defining. Even Yahveh (in his popular King James aspect), when pressed to define himself, had recourse to a tautology: "I Am that I Am."

We have seen that communication is as important to meaningful expression as "extension" is. And communication is only possible through the sharing of associations derived from certain conventional contexts among those who wish to communicate. It follows that *some* conventional associations, and, by implication, the contexts that provide them, must be a part of every meaningful expression. The shared associations serve to *relate* the meaningful qualities of the expression to the lives and orientations of those who communicate; without this relational character those meaningful qualities, however provocative, would not be understood or appreciated. And so every communicating human enterprise, every community, every "culture," is strung on a relational framework of conventional contexts. These are never *absolutely* conventionalized, in the sense of being identical for all who share them; they are always loose-ended, incompletely shared, in process of change, and they may or may not be consciously learned, in the sense of "rules." But the rather tenuous and poorly understood thing that we speak of optimistically as "communication" is only possible to the degree that associations *are* shared.

In every "culture," every community or communicating human enterprise, the range of conventional contexts is centered around a generalized image of man and human interpersonal relationships, and it articulates that image. These contexts define and create a meaning for human existence and human sociality by providing a *collective* relational base, one that can be actualized explicitly or implicitly through an infinite variety of possible expressions. They include such things as language, social "ideology," what is called "cosmology," and all the other relational sets that anthropologists delight in calling "systems" (though of course their "systematic" aspect is as important or unimportant as one wants to make it). This does *not*, of course, mean that the ideal and its image of man is the same for all human cultures, or that they play the same part in every culture's view or scheme of the person and his action in the world, although the ways in which cultures differ in this regard are crucial to our understanding of them. The collective, conventional meanings of man and his sociality may be implicit or explicit aspects of human action, and hence of invention itself, but they are always there. And it was a central insight in the work of Emile Durkheim that\this collective image of man and human sociality in every culture comprises what we could call a field of morality.

> Everything which is a source of solidarity is moral, everything which forces man to take account of other men is moral, everything which forces him to regulate his conduct through something other than the striving of his ego is moral, and morality is as solid as these ties are numerous and strong.[1]

Morality is fully half of the world of meaning in this sense. And morality may help to clarify the mid-twentieth-century illusion that

1. Emile Durkheim, *The Division of Labor in Society,* tr. George Simpson (New York: The Free Press, 1966), p. 398.

human life can be meaningfully accounted for by talking about "systems," "coding," "norms," or "relationships." Morality is a kind of *meaning,* a meaning with direction, purpose, and motivation, rather than a systemic substratum. It is a cultural *construct,* a range of contexts built up out of the associations of other contexts, just as its own associations may serve in the articulation of still other constructions.

The moral or conventional contexts of a culture define and orient its meaningful expressions and those who construct them; they "pull the world together." They simultaneously *relate* expressive constructions and *are themselves* expressive constructions, creating an image and an impression of an absolute in a world that has no absolutes. Our problem, our task, and our interest in this chapter is to understand how this illusion is created, how it works and motivates itself, and how it maintains its preeminence in the course of action.

Control

Clearly, if words are just sounds and visual images just patterns of light, neither have innate or self-evident associations. We have seen that any associations they might take on are acquired through participation in various contexts. Yet it would be the purest tautology to say that a particular context takes its objective characteristics from itself or from the experiences that it structures. Since its articulating elements guide and channel our experience of its reality, they cannot take their form and character directly from that experience. It follows that these characteristics are given largely by the *other* associations of the elements that articulate the context, the ones that they acquire through participation in contexts external to the one in question. The various contexts of a culture get their meaningful characteristics from one another, through the participation of symbolic elements in more than one context. They are invented out of each other, and the idea that some of the recognized contexts in a culture are "basic" or "primary," or represent the "innate," or that their properties are somehow essentially objective or real, is a cultural illusion.

Yet it is a necessary illusion, as much a part of living in and inventing a culture from the "inside" as the anthropologist's assumption of hard and fast rules is a prop for his invention of the culture from the "outside." Meaningful expression is always a matter of using "props" of this sort, and therefore it always moves in a world of cultural illusion, one, moreover, which it continually "lays down" for itself, as a tank lays its own tracks. Our symbols do not relate to an external "reality" at all; at most they refer to other symbolizations, which we perceive as reality.

All human thought, action, interaction, perception, and motivation can be understood as a function of the construction of contexts drawing upon the contextual associations of symbolic (semiotic) elements. Since all such action, whether effective or ineffective, good or bad, "correct" or "incorrect," is developed through successive constructions, its generation can be described as "invention" or "innovation." The invention blends contextual associations into a complex product in a way that can be illustrated by the notion of "metaphoric" or "pragmatic" construction in linguistic usage. A metaphor embodies a new or innovative sequence, but it also changes the associations of the elements it brings together by making them part of a distinctive and often novel expression. Elsewhere I have used the term "metaphor" in reference to cultural invention,[2] though such use requires that we "metaphorize" the notion of metaphor, extending it to encompass nonverbal forms and hence developing a theory of symbolization on the analogy of language. I am, however, concerned with linguistic phenomena largely as an instance of more general semiotic operations, rather than vice versa, and thus I will cite the example of metaphor here for its illustrative value alone.

Conventional symbolizations are those that relate to one another within the field of discourse (language and mathematics are the obvious examples) and form cultural "sets," like sentences, equations, tool kits, suits of clothes, or city streets. They generalize or collectivize through their capacity to link commonly held signs together into a single pattern. But they can do this only because they label, or encode, the details of the world they order. All conventional symbolizations, to the degree that they are conventional, have the property of "standing for," or denoting, something other than themselves. This is the traditional notion of the "symbol," used by C. S. Pierce and others.

Thus a contextual contrast—between the symbolic context articulated by signs, and the context of phenomena to which those signs refer—is a feature of conventional symbolization wherever it occurs. The symbols *abstract themselves* from the symbolized. Because we are obliged to use symbols in order to communicate, and because these symbols must necessarily include more or less conventional associa-

2. Roy Wagner, *Habu: The Innovation of Meaning in Daribi Religion* (Chicago: The University of Chicago Press, 1972).

tions among the sum available, the effect of symbolic self-abstraction, and the consequent contextual contrast, is always a factor in symbolization.

In addition to giving the world a center, a pattern, and an organization, convention also separates its own ordering capabilities from the things ordered, or designated, and it creates and distinguishes contexts in the process. Although the delineation of these contexts and the opposition of "collectivizing" and "differentiating" modes of symbolization that it implies might both be treated as fictions or illusions of convention, they are extremely important ones. They parse the world of the actor, and of the tradition at large, into its most significant and effective categorizations.

The contrasting element to the conventional, that which is "represented" or "signified" by conventional symbolization (and which, of course, symbolizes it in turn), is not to be equated simply with the range of "self-evident" things in the world—individual people, places, events, etc.—although it certainly includes them. It is, in fact, another mode of symbolization: the differentiating, or nonconventional mode. Its effects are opposite, in virtually every respect, to those of the conventional mode, although they too can be understood in terms of semiotic properties.

When a symbol is used in some nonconventional way, as in the formation of a metaphor or some other sort of trope, a new referent is introduced simultaneously with the novel symbolization. Because neither signifier nor signified belongs to the established order of things, the act of symbolization can only be referred to an event—the act of invention in which form and inspiration come to figure each other. The result is no different for the symbolizations we apprehend in discovering a new face or a new situation—an event manifests symbol and referent simultaneously. Thus the tension and contrast between symbol and symbolized collapse, and we may speak of such a construction as a "symbol" that stands for itself." The unique experiences, people, objects, and places of everyday life all correspond, in those features that render them distinct, to this mode of symbolization—as "symbols," they stand for themselves.

The tendency of differentiating symbolism, therefore, is to impose radical, binding distinctions upon the flow of construction, to specify, and to assimilate to one another the contrasting contexts set up by convention. "Invention," the "sign" of differentiation, is the obviator of conventional contexts and contrasts; indeed, its total effect of merging the conventional "subject" and "object," transforming each on the basis of the other, might be labelled "obviation." The giving or taking of associations from one context to another is a consequence of this effect, one that I propose to call *objectification*. (My use of the term "objectify" here is somewhat phenomenological and resembles Nancy Munn's term "objectivate" in her discussion of Walbiri iconography, where she demonstrates how the imagery of Walbiri representation provides "objective correlates" for the "sensual formations of subjective experience.")[3]

A conventional symbolization objectifies its disparate context by bestowing order and rational integration upon it; a differentiating symbolization specifies and concretizes the conventional world by drawing radical distinctions and delineating its individualities. But since objectification is simply the effect upon the respective contexts of their merger, or obviation (as, indeed, the contexts themselves are merely delineations of conventional self-abstraction), the two "kinds" of objectification are necessarily simultaneous and reciprocal—the collective is differentiated as the individual is collectivized.

Because, given the nature of conventional symbolization, the collective must always "signify" the differentiating, and vice versa, and because, given the nature of differentiating symbolization, the action of one symbolic mode upon the other is always reflexive, all symbolic effects are mobilized in any given symbolization. It is impossible to objectify, to invent something, without "counterinventing" its opposite. Of course, a realization of this fact by the symbolizer would be deadly to his intention: to see the whole field at once, in all its implications, is to suffer a "relativization" of intention, to become aware of how gratuitous a part it plays in the activation of symbols. Thus the most compelling necessity of action under these circumstances is a restriction of vision, concentrating the awareness and intention of the actor upon one of the modes and its effect.

Control of this sort is provided by the sharp and binding ideological discrimination made between the two symbolic modes in all human traditions. Either the conventional mode abstracts itself out as the proper realm of human action, leaving the differentiating mode as the realm of the innate, or given, or else the conventional abstracts itself off *as* the innate, and thus designates differentiation as the mode appropriate to human action. In either case, the differential weighting and moral emphasis given respectively to the two modes will serve

3. Nancy D. Munn, *Walbiri Iconography: Graphic Representation and Cultural Symbolism in a Central Australian Society* (Ithaca and London: Cornell University Press, 1973), p. 221.

to control the attention of the symbolizer, masking their essentially symbolic nature and their obviating reflexivity. As we shall see, the consequences and motivations will be very different, depending on whether the symbolizer goes "with" or "against" the conventional prescriptions for action; from the standpoint of control and masking, however, all that matters is that the two realms be kept sufficiently distinct.

I shall speak of the context upon which the attention of a symbolizer is focused, regardless of its ideological status, as the *control,* or *controlling context,* for it is this context and this symbolic mode that controls his attention by restricting the field of awareness. I shall speak of the opposite mode, that which is "taken" or acted upon, as the *implicit context.* The effect of *masking,* of restricting the actor's intention and awareness in this way, is to involve them, not only in the action itself, but also in the judgments and priorities of the conventional world.

For masking is nothing more than the conditioning of our awareness by the self-abstracting property of conventional symbols. Whether they are used to build up a conventionally recognized context or are drawn upon in deliberate acts of obviation, conventional symbols are *there,* and their effect of distinguishing the contexts, subject from object, will necessarily be part of the whole action, perceived or intended, as the case may be. When the control is a differentiating one, however, the masking separation of contexts will be manifest as an intrusion upon the intention, like a guilty conscious, for the force of differentiating acts is to bring about a union of subject and object, and the intention of the symbolizer seeks a kind of unmasking, the obviation of the subject-object dichotomy. The "psychological" aspect of symbolization results from the separation, incorporated within the awareness of the symbolizer, between collectivizing and differentiating, and between masking and obviation—a separation that is necessary if he is to be shielded from the essential relativism of all symbolic construction.

Because it involves the combination or mutual articulation of two contexts, every act of cultural invention results in two kinds of objectification. Both are, of course, consequences and aspects of a single, complex act, and each represents the significance of that act in terms of a particular part of the conceptual world. The particular control that the actor is using causes him to regard one kind of transformation or objectification as the *result* of his own intentions, what he is "doing." He identifies the *other* kind of objectification, that which transforms the controlling context itself and which we might call "counterinvention," with the *cause* or *motivation* of his intentions. This observation may seem puzzling or far-fetched at first, but it should be clear that the transformation of the control is easily perceptible *in relation to* the action, and since it is not part of the actor's intention, it is invariably associated with some innate motivational or external compulsion, that which is "causing" the intention.

This, too, is a cultural illusion, and a consequence of the phenomenon of masking. And yet if the source of motivation is an illusion, its motivating effect is not, for by committing himself to the control as a course of action, the actor makes himself vulnerable to the illusions of masking that such action brings upon him. It is an illusion with teeth in it. We might better understand how the illusion operates by returning to the fact that every meaningful invention must involve both a conventional and a nonconventionalized context, one of which "controls" the other, and by exploring the implications of this fact.

When the conventional context is the one that serves as the control, the actor is focusing on an articulation of things that conforms to some sort of cultural (and moral) convention. He is acting in explicit conformity with some collectively held ideal or expectation of the way in which things "should be done," constructing his context along lines that correspond to a shared image of the moral and the social. His action might be explained as "following the rules," or explicitly trying to be moral, but in any case he is collectivizing his action. That is, he is controlling his act in accordance with a kind of model that signifies the "holding together" of society and morality, building consistency and social cohesion. But of course since the *other* context, the one in which he acts in this collectivizing way, is *not* a conventional one, the resulting construction will include both conventional (moral) and nonconventionalized (particular) characteristics—it will be "like" the actor's intentions in some ways, and "different from" them in others. The actor, following his intentions, will have succeeded in "collectivizing" the context of his action to some extent, transforming a woods into a garden, or a group of people into a family or nation. He will have recreated and carried forth some nonconventionalized context (a particular woods, a certain bunch of individuals) in conventional form, transforming it into "culture" or "morality." But he will also have re-created and carried forth a conventional context (the "rules" or accepted techniques for making a garden, or a family, or a nation) to some degree in particularistic or nonconventional form. The masking that accompanies his action will cause him to view these two resulting kinds of objectification in different ways.

Suppose I try to treat my wife "as a husband should" by following some shared set of cultural expectations as a control, hoping to transform our association into "a marriage" and "a family." The nonconventionalized context of my action will be the individual personal, social, and situational characteristics of my wife and I, and those of our previous association. By focusing my action on "being a good husband," and thereby focusing hers on "being a good wife," I participate in a common activity of "building a marriage" and "building a family." To the degree that our efforts are successful, we will transform an interaction between individuals into something like the conventional notions of "marriage" and "family." Since we both belong to a culture that holds some fairly distinct notions of what "marriage" and "family" should be, and since in controlling our actions we have focused on these notions, we will be under the illusion that the complex product of our invention is a real thing. And because of our commitment to that thing, the *other* kind of objectification that is going on, *as a direct consequence of our action,* will appear as a natural process, a consequence of "what we are," of "our own (individual and collective) way of doing it."

Thus the objectification of the control—in this case a conventional context—will be masked by our identification of our intentions with that control. Though they are made apparent, and to that extent *created* as a cultural context, by our actions, we do not see these personal and situational characteristics as the result of those actions. Furthermore, since the tendency of this objectification—which is to particularize rather than collectivize—*runs directly counter to that of our intentions,* it is perceived as a kind of resistance to them. Where we strive to transform our idiosyncracies and diverse situations into something like a moral and social ideal, these idiosyncracies and situations are simultaneously impinging upon that ideal and changing its shape and its semblance, creating a resistance to our intentions. But this resistance also has the effect of "setting up" situations for further collectivizing by always partially undoing whatever we set out to do: it has the effect of *motivating* our collectivization. Since we recognize it as part of our "natural selves," it appears in the form of natural motivation, sex drives, personal fixations, inbuilt talent or propensity—what we "are" and what we "do to" each other. Of course, the more we act according to our collectivizing intentions, the more solidly we build up an impression of this impinging resistance *as a continuous force* motivating our action. By inventing the culturally prescribed collectivities, we counterinvent our notion of a "given" world of natural facts and motivations.

When the nonconventionalized context is the one that serves as the control, the actor is focusing on an articulation of things that differs in some ways from the conventions of social (and moral) expectation. When one particular control is selected from other possible or permissible ones, the meaningful construct that is produced becomes distinctive and individual. Instead of collectivizing the individual and particular, the actor is particularizing and differentiating the collective and the conventional. He is "doing his own thing," following one particular course of action in a situation (i.e., the shared conventions of society) that admits of other alternative courses, and thereby making what he does distinctive and individual. Instead of "following the rules" and focusing on consistency and cohesion, he is deliberately "trying" or "extending" the "rules" by building the world of situations and particulars to which they apply. But since the context of his action, the thing (i.e., "rules," conventions) that he is differentiating, *is* collective and conventionalized, the resulting construction will include both conventional and nonconventionalized (particular) characteristics. It will be "like" his intention in some ways and "different from" it in others. In his own eyes, the actor will have succeeded in "differentiating" the context of his action to some extent, transforming a common language or social code into his unique utterance, or poem, or party. He will have re-created and carried forth some conventional context in individual form, transforming it into "his" or "his kind of" life. But he will also have re-created and carried forth a nonconventionalized context ("his own way" of writing a poem, or having a party) to some extent in a collective or conventional form. And of course the masking that accompanies his action will result in his viewing these two resulting kinds of objectification in different ways.

Suppose that instead of treating my wife "as a husband should," I decide to act "as a man," to differentiate my actions from hers on the model of some kind of masculinity. In the context of our being married, with all its conventional arrangements and expectations, I will try to make what I do consciously different from what she does, and thus create my individuality as a person and a man. (This would of course be regarded as "forced" and unnatural in middle-class American life, because sex drives and personality traits are supposed to be "given" and natural.) By focusing my action on "being a man" or "being an individual" and separating her efforts from mine ("don't burden me with womanly things"), I deliberately try to create the personal and situational factors that surround our marriage. She may or may not go along with this program, but whether she tries frustratedly to collectivize, or attempts to play "woman" to my "man," I shall manage to differentiate. To the degree that I am successful I will transform a marriage into an interaction between individuals. Since I am controlling my action with a specific contextual pattern in mind, I will be under the illusion that the complex product of this invention is a real transformation. And because of my commitment to that transformation, the other kind of objectification that is going on, the collectivizing of my differentiating control, will appear to me as something impinging from the outside, a "given" that is not a part of my intention.

I will, of course, counterinvent the collective context of our marriage in the very act of individuating myself against it. And since I am trying to differentiate, to create my individuality, this collectivizing counterinvention will be perceived as a kind of resistance to my intentions, a motivating factor that continually "sets things up" for further acts of differentiation. But in this instance I cannot attribute the motivating force to my "natural self," since the conventions of my culture teach me that the natural "givens" are individual and particularizing, whereas this motivation is social and collectivizing. So, although the motivation is actually created and made apparent in the course of control, the kinds of objectification that it leads to are not considered "normal" in my culture, and are assumed to be pathological. I perceive them as vague, inexplicable "compulsions" bearing upon my activity and forcing me to differentiate more and more. Insofar as I depend upon nonconventionalized controls, I will perceive (and counterinvent) my culture as a compulsion in this way. If I lived in a culture where nonconventionalized controls are considered normal, I would perceive this collective compulsion as my "soul." If I were a criminal in this society, its pathological nagging would draw me onward to greater and greater crimes. But I am only a harmless scholar, with an obsessional culture that wishes to free itself by being written into more and more books.

Between the two kinds of objectification the whole world is invented—one of its aspects motivating the other, or vice versa. But the whole matter of which *kind* of objectification is considered the normal and appropriate medium of human action (the realm of human artifice) and which is understood as the workings of the innate and "given" plays an important part in this. It defines the accepted and conventional form of human action, the way in which the actor interprets and experiences control and its illusions, and thus it also defines what things and what experiences are to be regarded as prior to his actions and *not* a result of them. We might call this collective orientation the "conventional masking" of a particular culture. In the modern American middle-class Culture of science and collective enterprise, with its emphasis on the progressive and artificial building up of collective forms, conventional masking amounts to an understanding that the world of natural incident (the sum of all nonconventionalized contexts) is innate and given. And in the world of the Daribi and of Yali's people, with its stress on the priority of human relationships, it is the incidental realm of nonconventionalized controls that involves human action, whereas the articulation of the collective is the subject of counterinvention and conventional masking.

Yali's culture and the culture of the Daribi are innate and motivating, they "want to be" extended and differentiated against; it is a part of their conventional character that they should be normally counterinvented through the use of differentiating controls. But American Culture is artificial and imposed; it is the heritage of many generations of progress, of builders and creators who, motivated by "nature" themselves, developed our techniques of mastering, applying, and regulating nature. In the first instance, cultural convention masks its own invention as motivation; in the second, its conscious articulation masks the invention of an innate and motivating nature. Thus conventional masking is always carried forth and re-created as a part of the operation of invention itself: it is implicit in the conventional contexts themselves, as they are invented or counterinvented. And its continual re-creation motivates, or is motivated, in the same way that these contexts are.

If this is true, how can we account for acts that invert the culturally appropriate order of control, the deliberate differentiation that occurs in American Culture, and the collectivization that takes place in New Guinea? Since these inversions counteract the ordinary creation of motivations, we cannot attribute them to the illusions of conventional masking. They are in fact a kind of "unmasking," doing the things one is ordinarily not able to do, and although they do create their own motivation in the form of compulsion, the impetus for such a "reversal" of action remains to be explained. If we can account for this, it might also help us to understand why it is that the conventional modes of acting and the illusions they create remain conventional. For the assertion that actions create their own motivations tells us little indeed about how this state of affairs comes about, or where it is going. The existence of a conventional mode of action and of masking poses a problem that cannot be solved by the notion of control alone, and this is the problem of the necessity of invention.

The necessity of invention

The contexts of culture are perpetuated and carried forth by acts of objectification, by being invented *out of each other* and *through each other*. This means that we cannot appeal to the force of something called "tradition," or "education," or spiritual guidance to account for cultural continuity, or for that matter cultural change. The symbolic associations that people share in common, their "morality," "culture," "grammar," or "customs," their "traditions," are as much dependent upon continual reinvention as the individual idiosyncrasies, details, and quirks that they perceive in themselves or in the world around them. Invention perpetuates not only the things we "learn," like language and good manners, but also the regularities of our perception, like color and sound, and time and space themselves. Since the collective and conventional only makes sense in relation to the individual and idiosyncratic, and vice versa, collective contexts can only be retained and recognized as such by being continually drawn through the meshes of the individual and the particular, and the individual and particular characteristics of the world can only be retained and recognized as such by being drawn through the meshes of the conventional. Order and disorder, known and unknown, conventional regularity and the incident that defies regularity, are tightly and innately bound together, they are functions of each other and necessarily interdependent. We cannot act but that we invent each through the other.

If *invention* is thus crucially important to our realization of action and the world of action, then *convention* is no less so, for cultural convention defines the perspective of the actor. Without invention, the world of convention, with its all-important interpretive distinction of the "innate" and the "artificial," could not be carried forth. But without the conventional distinctions that orient the actor in his world, that tell him who he is and what he may do and so give his acts a conventional masking and a conventional motivation, invention would be impossible. The core of any and every set of cultural conventions is a simple distinction as to what kind of contexts, the nonconventionalized ones or those of convention itself, are to be deliberately articulated in the course of human action, and what kind of contexts are to be counterinvented as "motivation" under the conventional mask of "the given" or "the innate." Of course, for any given set of conventions, be it that of a tribe, community, "culture," or social class, there are only two possibilities: a people who deliberately differentiate as the form of their action will invariably counterinvent a motivating collectivity as "innate," and a people who deliberately collectivize will counterinvent a motivating differentiation in this way. As contrasting modes of thought, perception, and action, there is all the difference in the world between these two.

Thus the collective viewpoint or orientation of a culture, the way in which its members learn to experience action and the world of action, is always a matter of convention. It persists through being constantly reinvented in the form of conventional contexts. But the means by which this viewpoint is extended and reinvented is that of differentiation and particularization in terms of nonconventionalized contexts. The acts of expression that must necessarily articulate each kind of context together with the other in order to be both communicable and significant ensure their continual reinvention out of one another. It is an invention that constantly re-creates its orientation, and an orientation that continually facilitates its own reinvention. Identifying the orientation with the shared consistency of conventional associations, and the invention with the impinging contradiction of differentiating contrasts, we can conclude that the necessary interaction and interdependence between them is the most urgent and powerful necessity in human culture. *The necessity of invention is given by cultural convention, and the necessity of cultural convention is given by invention.* We invent so as to sustain and restore our conventional orientation; we adhere to this orientation so as to realize the power and gain that invention brings.

Invention and convention stand in a *dialectical* relationship to one another, a relationship of simultaneous interdependence and contradiction. This dialectic is the core of all human (and very likely all animal) cultures. The concept of "dialectic" may well be familiar to readers in its Hegelian and Marxist formulation as a historical process or working out involving a succession of thesis, antithesis, and synthesis. My formulation, much less explicit typological, is both simpler and, I think, closer to the original Greek idea—that of a tension or dialogue-like alternation between two conceptions or viewpoints that are simultaneously contradictory and supportive of each other. As a way of thinking, a dialectic operates by exploiting contradictions (or, as Lévi-Strauss would call them, "oppositions") against a common ground of similarity, rather than by appealing to consistency against a common ground of differences, after the fashion of rationalistic or "linear" logic. It follows that cultures that conventionally differentiate approach things with a dialectical "logic," whereas those that conventionally collectivize (like our own rationalistic tradition) invoke a linear causality. Because I wish to stress the necessary presence and interdependence of both conventional and nonconventionalized contexts, I shall speak of a meaningful and collectively binding dialectic (convention plus invention), where anthropologists have generally spoken of convention plus natural force or convention plus evolution.

Although its content, and sometimes its relation to the actor, may change, this binding dialectic never becomes more or less than a dialectic. It has its own continuity built into it; whichever aspect an actor chooses as the control on his actions, whether he collectivizes or differentiates, he will counterinvent and "set up" the other aspect.

Convention, which integrates an act into the collectivity, serves the purpose of drawing collective distinctions between the innate and the realm of human action. Invention, which has the effect of continually differentiating acts and events from the conventional, continually puts together ("metaphorizes") and integrates disparate contexts. And the cultural dialectic, which necessarily includes both of these, becomes a universe of integrating distinctions and distinctive integrations, drawing people together by resolving their continuous action into "the innate" and "the artificial," and distinguishing individual persons, acts, and events by combining innate and artificial contexts in novel and highly specific ways.

Consider what happens when we speak. Often it seems to me that members of a highly literate civilization like our own imagine spaces between the words they use when they talk, rather like those that appear between words on the printed page. (Indeed, they seem to imagine the words themselves, as well as their punctuation.) In fact, what we produce in speech is a kind of blurred and mumbly music, and one has to learn how to resolve this orchestration into conventional forms and units if one is to make sense of it, much as a trained musician learns to resolve a roar of sensuous tonality into notes, chords, harmony, melodic line, and structural form. It does not really matter *what* the conventions themselves are like, whether one is literate, what aspect of the total production is conventionally visible (I often suspect that my Daribi friends resolve speech into *things* and *intentions* rather than words and sentences); what matters, insofar as communication is concerned, is whether the speaker (who is, of course, listening to his own music) and the listener make the same resolutions. If convention plays the critic's role in this endlessly concerted human performance, then invention is the composer. For us, the composer happens to be "innate," like some subterranean and incomprehensible Beethoven, whereas for the Daribi and other tribal peoples it is the critic that is innate.

Invention changes things, and convention resolves those changes into a recognizable world. But neither the distinctions of convention nor the operations of invention can be identified with some fixed "mechanism" within the human mind, or with some kind of superorganic "structure" imposed upon the human situation. All that we ever have is a set of orderings and articulations, relatively more or less conventionalized for every actor, which action represents to us in absolute terms as innate and artificial, conventional and nonconventionalized. We participate in this world through its illusions, and *as* its illusions. The inventions in which it is realized are only rendered possible through the phenomenon of control and the masking that accompanies it, and the conventional distinctions in which control is grounded can only be carried forth by being re-created in the course of invention.

Because convention can only be carried forth through a process of change, it is inevitable that its conventional distinctions will suffer change in the course of it. Moreover, since invention is always a matter of combining conventional contexts with the particular and the non-conventionalized, deliberately collectivizing the particular and individualistic or differentiating the collective, it is apparent that either kind of action will result in a progressive "relativization" of both, particularizing the collective as it orders and collectivizes the particular. We apply the conventional orders and regularities of our science to the phenomenal world ("nature") in order to rationalize and understand it, and in the process our science becomes more specialized and irrational. Simplifying nature, *we* take on its complexity, and this complexity appears as an *internal* resistance to our intention. Invention inevitably confounds the distinctions of convention by relativizing them.

This is, of course, the phenomenon of motivation as we encountered it in our discussion of control. Motivation is the effect upon an actor of the reflexive objectification (and relativizing) of his control, a resistance to his intentions that has no obvious origin in his intentions themselves. Thus motivation always arises from the relativizing of conventional distinctions, from the differences between the contexts that an actor recognizes and those he produces, and *the tendency of motivation is always to oppose and counter the relativizing of conventional distinctions*. Ultimately, motivation is simply the inertia or the felt necessity of having to resolve things in a certain way.

It is important to note that motivation, although linked to action, does not necessarily originate "within" the individual. It is a part of the world of convention and illusion in which we participate and act, but not, apart from the necessary illusions of the actor himself, a "thing" or force emanating from the actor. Objects, pictures, memories, and other people motivate us quite as much as we motivate ourselves, and indeed our personalities constantly interpenetrate the theater of our actions and perceptions. It is only cultural convention, though a motivated convention at that, that resolves the situations of our action and invention into the cultural boundaries of individuals, "movements," guiding spirits, or into the culturally appropriate forms of "drives," "instincts," "the soul," and so on. Motivations can be "set up" by what one does, by what others do, by a situation in which one finds oneself, and the form and source of the motivation is always a function of the conventional distinctions through which these things are interpreted.

Motivation, then, is the way in which the actor perceives the relativizing of convention, and hence of the conventional contexts through which conventional distinctions are realized. We learn language, social interaction, roles, skills, and creativity as a part of relating to others, beginning with the family and extending outward to playmates, friends, mates, enemies, associates, and even casual encounters. We learn to act, to orient ourselves, and hence learn our motivations, in manifold contexts that include a bewildering array of general and particular elements, people, places, objects, situations, and institutions. Because this learning always occurs as an aspect of relating to others, it follows that the individual never simply learns to act or motivate himself as a "neutral" or uncommitted response. He learns to do so from a particular standpoint, to objectify through a particular focus, and thus he learns to identify different modes of his action with conscious intent and unconscious motivation. He learns a conventional orientation as a result of inventing, but he also learns to invent by using controls in some conventional relationship, one that renders him vulnerable to the illusions of motivation. Invention is always a kind of "learning," and learning is invariably an act of invention, or reinvention—to the point where it does us little good to speak of learning as a "process," or to divide it up into "stages." A child is as much a participant in the dialectic of invention and convention as an adult (at most his memory is a bit shorter), and it says little to assert that he lives in "a different world." We all live in different worlds.

What happens, then, for any given actor, when the relativization, and thus the motivating resistance, of the control he is using overpowers its effectiveness in terms of his original intention? Or, to put it differently, how do we react to highly relativized controls, whether used by ourselves or by others? The answer is that the action (and intention) invalidates itself; it aligns the actor's or reactor's controlling focus with the "resistance" to the control rather than with the original control, with the thing being counterinvented rather than the intended transformation of it. In doing so it engenders a sharp, motivated reaction against the original intention. This reaction is a part of *experience,* a kind of antipathy or frustration that the individual must learn to accommodate and deal with as he learns to accommodate the other aspects of motivation. For such a sudden surge of inverse motivation is as much a part of the necessity to resolve action in a conventional way as any other manifestation of motivation: it is born of the perception that one is going against the nature of things.

The best example I can think of is the familiar reaction of an audience to a bad pun, or a performance that appears "faked" and betrays the highly charged interplay of reality and construction that onlookers expect. The reaction is often as crude and upsetting as an outburst of anger, for it has the same roots; in every respect it is an *uncontrolled* reaction. And it is accessible to children as well as adults, for learning this reaction is concomitant with the learning of convention in the course of invention, and vice versa. In the case of the pun, the audience reacts to the relativizing of language, its ambiguity (for language is as much motivated and motivating as any other part of culture); in that of a theatrical or motion picture performance the audience reacts to the relativizing of a "play" situation in which it invested credulity in the expectation of certain "entertainment" rewards.

The reaction is of course by no means limited to jokes and entertainment circumstances; it lies at the root of all the acts we associate with "negative" or "destructive" behavior, including much of the crime and vandalism that beset our highly relativized urban Culture, and the depredations that people so often visit upon "foreigners" who seemingly mock their way of doing things. As a mere reaction, it is often incomprehensible to those who manifest it, though it is capable of infinite interpretation and rationalization *after the fact.* As an extreme form of restoring convention, as a crucial and recurrent actional turning point, it demands our closer attention.

Whatever the circumstances of its occurrence, the perception of the relativity of a controlling context amounts to an "unmasking" of the invention at hand, and to a feeling of "something being done" to those who participate. It is this feeling that triggers the negative reaction, especially in the onlookers or those who co-participate with the actor. They feel vulnerable and become defensive, they wish to "strike out" at the offending influence, and what they are defending is a certain conventional mode of perception and action. Since we have learned that this conventional mode can be reduced to an overriding distinction that identifies either the conventional contexts or a sum of nonconventionalized ones as "innate," and consigns the other to the realm of human manipulation, it turns out that two kinds of "unmasking" are possible within our own conventional universe. *When the controls on the ordinary mode of serious activity, what people "do," are relativized, the resulting invention appears "faked," "not serious," "just made up"; when the controls on the inverse mode of action, "creativity," "art," "research," "ritual," "play" or "recreation" are relativized, the resulting invention appears "forced," "com-*

mercialized," "*too serious,*" or "*sacreligious.*" In each case the transformation works counter to the one originally intended.

We can understand this better, and perhaps gain some insight into
the extreme relativization of our present society, if we draw some
examples from modern American life. Americans participate in a
conventional orientation that emphasizes the articulation of conventional contexts as the realm of human action, and recognizes the
"innate" (including the temporal and situational) as made up of
nonconventionalized contexts. But Americans complain more and
more of the "contrived" and "made up" quality of administrative
and technological solutions, of the superficial and unrewarding character of much of their work, and also of the manipulative nature of
advertising, the commercialization of sports, and the fact that "people
work so hard at having fun anymore." This is not to assert that these
complaints are without justification, though the contriving and the
manipulation and commercialization were doubtless as extensive in
the 1870s as in the 1970s; what has changed is our perception of these
things as abuses, and our reaction to them as abuses. We want the
government to step in and decommercialize football or regulate advertising, or we want investigators to step in and make the government
serious and responsible again. With all the insistence of inverse motivation, we want to *restore* things—our very utopias are natural paradises
of artificial fresh air, enforested high-rises and socio-cultural terrariums.
And, of course, there are always those who would stop short and
treasure the reaction for its own sake by smashing things and assaulting
people.

But even this response caters to a naturalistic illusion; the reaction
to relativization is no more "primitive" or "basic" than concerted
action to counteract such relativity—both are consequences of learning
conventions and protecting conventional distinctions. The reaction
itself is a kind of cue, which can be mastered and built into an impetus
for some more effective control of the situation. The human personality is an arrangement for the preservation of conventional distinctions through this kind of control, balancing motivation against
compulsion by managing the transitions between them, and society is
an arrangement among actors to the same purpose. This means that
what we call "self-control" in a personality (what Freud would call
"sublimating conflicts") and "smooth functioning" or some such in the
case of society is a trick of learning to respond to highly relativized
controls by inverting one's mode of action. If the conventional controls
of our Culture and technology are relativized, we "rebuild" or "recharge" them by consciously focusing upon the differentiating mode of

objectification, the one that we "normally" counterinvent, and instead counterinvent Culture. When I find that "acting as a husband should" leads to frustration and conflict, I invert my mode of action and consciously build my identity as a man and as an individual, *differentiating* my actions and so counterinventing the "family" (my interaction with my wife) as a compulsive motivation.

Husband and wife, anthropologist and informant, artist or entertainer and audience, "middle class" and upper or lower class, doctor and patient, and often the conflicting components of an individual's personality, play constantly at this game of rebuilding and restoring the ambience of the other's action. It is a battle against relativization that *has to be* fought, for the convenional and its nonconventionalized background do not persist of themselves but must be continually invented out of each other, and this invention leads inevitably to relativization of the controls. It is the necessity of invention, and it is what interaction is all about, whether the interaction takes place among individuals and other constructs such as classes and institutions or within them.

We may describe all of this simply in terms of contexts. When we use contexts in the act of invention, we simultaneously reinvent them, and we reinvent the distinctions that they embody. In so doing we continually reinvent our interpretation of them, and so reinterpret our invention. The interpretation is completely dependent on the invention, and the invention is completely dependent upon the interpretation. But invention means that the controlling context takes on characteristics of the controlled context, and vice versa. The collective is always being differentiated and particularized on the model of the situations and idiosyncracies that it pulls together, and the individual and situational is constantly being collectivized and conventionalized on the model of the regularities it differentiates. Contexts that are continually articulated together tend to permeate one another and thus relativize one another: in the course of objectification, they exchange characteristics.

The only way this tendency may be counteracted is by inverting one's mode of action and reinventing the ordinary controls by objectifying them *in terms of novel or unusual situations and circumstances*. This inversion is always a matter of *invention* prompted by *convention;* it restores or sustains a conventional distinction or interpretation of what is innate and what is artificial and manipulable by changing the objective "content," the characteristics and associations, of the cultural contexts. In cultures like our own, which stress the deliberate articulation of conventional contexts, these collectivizing controls are re-created by acts of *differentiation,* deliberate invention. In tribal societies and others that emphasize the deliberate articulation of nonconventionalized contexts, the differentiating controls are re-created by acts of *collectivization,* deliberate conventionalizing. In the latter case, the need for novelty is met by *reformulating* the conventional contexts from time to time on the part of prophets, cult-leaders, or "lawgivers," or by the importation of exotic cults that is such an obvious part of the life of tribal peoples. We live our lives by ordering and rationalizing, and re-create our conventional controls in creative swoops of compulsive invention; tribal and religious peoples live by invention in this sense (which makes them so provocative and *interesting* to us), and revitalize their differentiating controls from time to time in bursts of hysterical conventionalizing.

For Americans this means that the elements that figure importantly in their collective Culture, those of kin relationship, law, the state, technology, and so forth must be continually charged with associations drawn from areas *outside* of our ordinary control of nature. The dialectic of Culture and nature must be "opened out" to include other realms of experience if it is to retain its meaningful objectivity and avoid becoming tautologous and moribund. We generally experience this as a need for recreation, play, art, or research—"getting more facts," "looking at things differently," "letting ourselves go," or "communing with nature." Our novels, plays, and movies place familiar relationships (like "love," "parenthood," "tolerance," "democracy") in exotic, historical, dangerous, or futuristic situations, both to control those situations and make them meaningful and to recharge the relationships themselves. Research and the quest for knowledge also has this double effect, giving our symbols objective associations in the process of "ordering" new frontiers of knowledge, and the vacationer "re-creates" his everyday life by seeking exotic contexts. In all cases Culture is invented by experiencing and creating the reality from which it takes its objective characteristics.

The necessity of invention is provided by the dialectic and the interdependence it necessitates among the various contexts of culture. Because we "use up" our symbols in the course of using them, we must forge new symbolic articulations if we are to retain the orientation that makes meaning itself possible. Our collective Culture creates and sustains an image and a perception of "nature" and natural force, whereas our compensating search for experience and knowledge in non-Cultural realms amounts to an invention of Culture. Living in and relying upon Culture creates the need for knowledge and experience of "nature" (including "human nature" and impulse); observing and experiencing nature makes Culture meaningful and necessary. The necessity may be masked as the need to constrain internal drives and external "forces of nature," or conversely as a need for relaxation, "getting away from it all," or discovering new facts, but in actuality it is a property of the dialectic through which meaning is and *must be* continually reinvented.

The tendency of culture is to sustain itself, by inventing itself. But I have observed that the conventional controls of modern American Culture are highly relativized—as ordering and unifying devices they are themselves disordered and particularized: our science and our technology are highly specialized, our administrative functions are hopelessly bureaucratized, our national symbols are nothing if not ambivalent. Culture is ambiguous (and anthropology exists to a large extent by exploiting that ambiguity). Furthermore, this did not come about as a result of Communists stealing our vital fluids, lax discipline, despoilers despoiling The Environment, Young People Ungrateful for Their Education, or "the mechanic rioting for a cheap loaf," though some of these are important symptoms. It results directly from the fact that we cling to our Culture, its proud traditions, its powerful techniques, its history and literature, its impressive rows of Great Names, over and above all attempts to reinvent it. We do not recast our Culture and its history completely every so often and slip over into a limbo of total re-creation, because we love our Culture so much. We try to remake it again and again, and look what we get!

Although nothing is going to make me stop loving Mozart, Beethoven, and the Salomon Symphonies of Haydn, this insistence on Culture, and the relativization that it entails, forces Americans to live in a continual frustration of solutions that fall apart in their very hands, and a continual tension of "wanting to do something about" things. It is a tension and frustration that infuses our moral, social, political, economic, and intellectual lives. In many ways it is the most important thing about America. This makes our efforts at "doing something about it" and inventing Culture doubly important and doubly interesting, for all the fact that they are bound to fail in certain respects. Let us explore them.

The magic of advertising

The problem of making our own Culture meaningful, of inventing its ideas and institutions, so to speak, and incorporating them within the ambient of everyday life, is dealt with in modern America by what I shall call "interpretive culture." Since the phenomenon has many manifestations, and is continually growing and changing, this term is only suggested as a matter of convenience. It includes what others have characterized as "popular culture," "mass culture," "the media," and "counterculture." The specific manifestations are ubiquitous: journalism, advertising, the "entertainment world," certain forms of art and education, popular religion, and the whole modality of interpretation known variously as "protest culture," "counterculture," "youth culture," "freak culture," "*the* subculture," and so on. All of these inventive "styles" base their relevance and their effectiveness on an imitation of orthodox Culture,[4] subsuming its forms as their "language" and thus depending upon its authority for the impact they make.

The success of this "imitation of Culture" (as measured in the current budgets, for instance, of the advertising and entertainment industries) can be attributed to its effectiveness in catering to the tensions of a highly relativized Culture. The work of simplifying, interpreting, or explaining, whether attempted by an artist or scientist, or for commercial or polemic reasons, becomes a reinvention of the subject. The increment, the "product" of advertising, journalism, entertainment, or even protest, is meaning, as well as the power over "reality" that the creation of meaning confers. Thus much of the commercial, imaginative, political, and even "esthetic" life of the country feeds upon the interpretive transformation of "straight" or orthodox ideology, and the latter is sustained by this very dialectic. Just as Culture, in the orthodox view, aims at the "mastery" or "interpretation" of nature, so these efforts undertake the mastery or interpretation of Culture, a remaking of human impulse and response that in turn affects the traditional ways of dealing with impulse and response.

"Interpretive culture" provides a meaningful context for the living of everyday life. It creates and provides for a particular audience, and develops a metaphoric approximation of Culture at large as its rationale. Journalism, for instance, addresses itself to its "public," however this may be conceived, and presents this public with an image of current history called "the news," a kind of serialized, factual worldpicture. The news draws its authority from the significance we attach to history, yet it is not history in the orthodox sense, but a reporting of events as if they were viewed from the perspective of an idealized history. The resultant air of objectivity serves journalism and the news industry as an *esprit de corps*. The entertainment world, on the other hand, is all the more interpretive for the fact that the image of life it

4. Thus we define "popular music" as that which, unlike "classical music," admits of interpretive changes according to the performer's "style." When a piece by Beethoven, Rossini, or Rimsky-Korsakov is "interpreted" by resetting the words, retooling the orchestration, we say that it has been "popularized," "jazzed up," that it is now a "popular" piece.

projects is one of fantasy; its caricature, mimicry, and dramatization succeeds as the very opposite of sober "fact." It interprets through the actor's, singer's, or comedian's license to "be" what others may not be, and its "personalities" in their everyday lives are surrounded by the aura of this metaphoric "being." (Stars sometimes have daydreams in which they are ordinary people.) The "show business" tradition incorporates (rather self-consciously) something of the same aura, that of professional interpretation through fantasy.

Popular religion, with its "congregations," its "sinners," and its "Bible," and counterculture, with its ideologies and communities of devotees, offer other examples of the interpretive invention of Culture. The aspect I have chosen to discuss, however, is that of advertising, the fabrication of a commercial "culture." Advertising is of special interest because it "creates" technology through personal effect; it aims at the kind of spurious conventionalization that we call "popularity" in order to sell its product. In fact, it is a short cut, an "instant culture" based on the insight that however clever a device may be, however crucial a technological advance it represents, it is useless and unmarketable unless applied in a meaningful way to the lives of people.

Advertising makes technology—in the form of special products with *very* special attributes—meaningful; it interprets them by creating for its audience a life that includes them. It does this by objectifying the products and their qualities through the means of personal impulses, situations, likes and dislikes. The strategies of advertising "borrow" from the moods and encounters, the annoyances and little gestures "that are so important," and the familiar and frustrating episodes of everyday life. They objectify attributes or qualities of a product in terms of this situational imagery, thus bestowing its associations on the product and insinuating the latter into a projection of everybody's everyday life.

In this respect advertising operates as a kind of inverse or "backwards" technology; it uses the intended effects of a product on peoples' lives, and human reactions to those effects, to build a meaningful identity for the product. It is possible to prove conclusively that any kind of pill or gadget "works better" than others, to make it "work better," provided only that we readjust our standards for how it should work. And this is how advertising itself works; it subtly redefines what kind of results people "want" by talking about its products in terms of those wants. If it succeeds in "selling" those wants and the quality of life they imply, it also "sells" the product that those wants and that life objectify.

Success depends upon the ability to objectify convincingly, to talk about the product in terms of other things in such a way that those other things seem to be qualities of the product. In this way advertising is like the "magic" of tribal peoples, which also objectifies productive activity through other imageries. Just as the meaning of products must be invented continually so that people will buy them, so that the products will not be taken for granted as ordinary details of life, so tribal peoples, for whom production is a part of family and kin life, must continually create a separate meaning and direction for their productive activity if it is not to become merely a mode of relating to people. If a Daribi gardener controlled his labors solely with the necessity of relating to his wife and her chores, there would be nothing to prevent him from doing sloppy, unproductive work. His effectiveness as a producer of food depends upon the creation of other, external meanings for his productive efforts. If he can control his production by focusing on these meanings, believing in their effectiveness, then his work of growing sweet potato (and therefore also his relations with his kinsmen) will stand to profit.

Thus he will often have recourse to magic "spells" designed (and believed) to make his work more effective. In the course of clearing and piling up brushwood in a newly cut garden, he may recite a spell that identifies his hands with the claws of a bushfowl, a bird that characteristically rakes forest debris into huge mounds to provide heat for the incubation of its eggs. The spell "works" ostensibly in the way that the bushfowl works, causing the user to be like the bushfowl in his ability to rake up brushwood. Its effectiveness, however, depends upon the user's belief in the spell and the significance of its transformation, for this will focus his activity on an ideal of bushfowl-like efficiency in the task of clearing brushwood; it will create his productiveness by creating its meaning, with a bushfowl as its "trademark."

One of the most frequently heard claims of advertising is that a product "works like magic." It works, in other words, like the advertising, the magic through which it is interpreted and introduced to the public. If this identity between the product and its advertised qualities is in fact maintained, if the redefined image of human wants, the style of life projected by the advertisement is accepted by the audience, then the product will fit into their lives as it fits into the lives projected by the ad. Advertisement sells its products by "selling" its objectification of the products, its image of a life that includes them. All one has to do is to believe the ad (like the magic spell): then one's acts will take on the focus of the advertiser and the product will "work like magic."

Suppose, for example, I want to sell automobile tires. From the standpoint of their conventional use, as necessary parts of a car, one tire is like another, and nothing could be more matter of fact than another old tire. If I want to sell my particular brand of tire, I must innovate upon this everyday significance of automobile tires by inventing a new meaning for tires and associating it with my brand. Thus the focus of my pitch will not be on automobile tires, any more than Daribi garden magic focuses on the ordinary social significance of gardening, or its techniques; I must *create* the meaning of my tire out of some other area of experience. If I want my tire to "sell," this meaning must be provocative, and the experience it draws upon should be a vivid and fascinating one to my audience.

I decide to objectify my tire through the world of auto racing, to create and control the meaning of my product by placing it within a context that has a very special significance for my audience. I might have drawn upon traffic safety and highway patrolmen, or the greasy consensus of tried and true garage mechanics, but I opt for a language that will metaphorize the thrill of motoring as well as safety and expertise. Auto racing as a sport has a power and fascination of its own; it is carried on by tough men with an air of expertise, men who risk their necks on their commitment to technology, and moreover do it for thrills as well as cash. They ought to know. What has this very frontier of camshafts and rpm's to say about tires? Amid the thrumming of engines and the squealing of brakes I have two or three crash-helmeted pros flash a quick repartee on the merits of my tire, which obviously has become part of the racing world.

Does this mean that the average Joe should take corners on two wheels, wear a crash helmet, and gun his engine as if he meant business? Hardly, anymore than a Daribi gardener finds it necessary to hop about and squawk like a bushfowl. It means that a tire that "works" under the demanding circumstances of auto racing will perform all the better in a family car, that my tire will bring all the expertise and toughness (and pleasure)—the "power" of auto racing to bear on the ordinary situations of driving. I have "made" the meaning of my tires by creating an image of the fun and power of driving, and by including these tires within the image.

As an interpretive medium, advertising is constantly remaking the meaning and experience of life for its audience, and constantly objectifying its products through the meanings and experiences it creates. Its interpretation of life often resembles or overlaps the interpretations put forth by other media—we have movies about auto racing, commercials in the form of newscasts and rock music performances. This is so because these media all share very much the same intent, that of investing the commonplace elements of life in unusual and provocative contexts, which give those elements new and powerful associations and recharge their conventional meanings. The profit realized by this kind of investment—in the form of popularity for one's product ("sales"), the number of books or tires or tickets sold—is a direct result of the increment of meaning created. It pays to be different, but what pays about the differences is that they are meaningful.

The life styles created and promoted by advertising involve technology in a continual dialectic with a collective image of the popular life, with the Culture of everyman. They precipitate this Culture anew. And the dialectic "inflates" life in the process of publicizing it; it makes its personal experiences and emotions commercially available to everyone (for a price) through the products that are sold, but it also has an effect upon those products. Instead of the relatively straightforward and "practical" devices of the last century, the products become adaptations to a "consumer world" of buying and selling, designed to "do the job" of selling well rather than that of curing headaches, cleaning teeth, or getting people from one place to another. The products "fit into" lives created by advertising, and one has to take part in those lives in order to use and enjoy the products. (This is what is meant by something being "in" or "out": a Culture that is heavily dependent upon reinterpretation for its survival becomes a thing of Culture-cult.) Just as the products are "sold" by being objectified through certain life styles, so they in turn objectify those life styles. They embody moods for the attuned consumer, and create episodes in his life, even though these are mere excrescences of the product's "magic." Moreover, since the items themselves are mass-produced, completely replaceable, or even intentionally perishable, they are virtually as communicable and conventionalized as words: others know exactly what you have bought, probably know why you bought it, and can get one just like it.

Technology used in this way has little enough to do with engineering and applied scientific law; together with the Culture it represents it is addressed to a manipulated "nature" of human contriving. Whatever else it does, it serves as a kind of analogue computer for the working out of peoples' lives. I could argue paradoxically that Americans are as little interested in technology for its own sake as Mexicans are interested in bulls or Geertz's Balinese in chickens.[5] Esthetes may compare a high-precision automobile engine to a Mozart concerto, hi fi enthusiasts may bore their friends with indescribably authentic reproductions of locomotives or thunderstorms, but both are in love with an ideal of precision and effectiveness rather than with the ma-

5. See Clifford Geertz, "Deep Play: Notes on the Balinese Cockfight," *Daedalus*, Journal of the American Academy of Arts and Sciences (Winter, 1972). Issue on "Myth, Symbol, and Culture."

chinery itself. Yet the love and the feeling could scarcely be experienced without the machinery, which gives them an objective presence, a dimension of highly specific attributes to serve both as their realization and as a means to further realizations.

Machines, gadgets, pills, and other products "do the work" of much of American society, or at least this is the way in which we normally think of them—as conveniences or clever "servants." They are "replacements" for man's physical and mental capabilities, his "natural" endowments, much as the bushfowl's claw is a replacement for the Daribi gardener's hands. As advertising continually redefines and re-creates the meaning of everyday life so as to include its products in that life, it also continually invests the products with new possibilities for helping people to lead meaningful lives. The product becomes the means by which the advertiser's magical vision of life can be the consumer's own life: all the consumer has to do is believe in the magic and buy the product. Then all the qualities and properties that the product has taken on in the context of the advertiser's presentation will be transferred to that of the consumer's personal life. The toothbrush, tire, or pill that is objectified in terms of human life style becomes in turn an objectifier for peoples' lives. Invested with the power and the thrill of the exotic or the "good life," it carries that power and that thrill into the everyday, refreshing and re-creating its meanings.

What advertising asks (and eventually compels) us to do is live in a world of technological "magic," where man-made wonders cure ills and make the daily round of life a continuing miracle, much as the Daribi tribesman lives in a magical world where human beings can take on the effectiveness of bushfowl or make it rain. Advertising invites us to make its magic our own. Just as the Daribi gardener must believe in the effectiveness of his spells if they are to successfully refocus his activity and bring real rewards, so the consumer must subscribe to a mystique of chemical and mechanical efficacy if his own "magic" is to realize its ends. The power focus of Daribi everyday life is on the force of words and arcane knowledge; that of American everyday life, for most people, is on the use of technology to solve their problems.

Unquestioningly, and at times quite unconsciously, we attribute all sorts of "natural" qualities to chemicals and machines, and then incorporate them in our tasks so as to make use of those qualities. Computers are said to have "intelligence": we put them to work figuring accounts and arranging dates; tanks and automatic weapons have destructive capacities: we fight our wars largely with them; drugs have power over the promised land of human physical makeup: we use them to augment the abilities of an allegedly physical "mind." Much of our thought and action amounts to a habitual objectification of human capacity—or of "nature" itself—in technological terms. We even think of living beings mechanistically as organic "systems," of creativity as "problem solving," and of life itself as a "process."

But a "naturalized" and particularized Culture, and an organized and systematized nature are part of a highly relativized world, one whose crucial distinction between "what we do" and "what we are" has been substantially eroded and broken down by the exchange of characteristics. The conventional forms of our Culture, including technology, differentiate and separate us almost as much as they unify a common control of "nature"; the particular and differentiating "nature" that surrounds (the Environment) and infuses (the behavioral human "system") us unifies as much as it draws distinctions. As a result, the objectification of each through the other is highly tautological: we systematize systems and particularize particulars. The frustration engendered by such a world, which can neither realize nor create its own meanings effectively, resolves quickly into a motivational apathy regarding Culture and its traditional perception of the "self" and a profound reaction of antipathy toward traditional solutions, a need to "do something about" things.

This is the need that requires and facilitates the commercial creation of needs that is advertising. Advertising requires both an apathy toward traditional Culture and a frustration of "wanting to do something about it" if it is to succeed. It draws upon them in projecting its image of what life *could* be and associating this image with its product. Like the yo-yo and trading card fad-world of kids, and like the perennial springtime of the cultists (who are always young however long their beards), advertising lives through the renewal of Culture. And so, like these cultist pursuits, it must continually precipitate an exaggerated and overly stodgy image of the conventional along with an exaggerated effectiveness of its own form of renewal. It counterinvents apathy and a humdrum world just as radicalism counterinvents the Establishment, cultism counterinvents "squares," and religious revivalism counterinvents Sin. This is the "progress" we live by, a progress that must constantly inflate, exaggerate, and create "the old" as a part of introducing "the new." It is the form, and the price, of hanging on to Culture.

Advertising is only one of the ways in which Americans must revitalize their Culture, and their commitment to Culture, if they are to have it at all. There is also "the news," journalism, entertainment, scientific and artistic exploration, messages from God, and the "dropout" world of people who want to live an inversion of Culture, as well as its many twilight zones. All of these have their "magic," all of them precipitate Culture—if only as the background of their hopes—and all of them are subject to much the same operating conditions. Even the government must get into the act. Advertising is merely the "socio-economic" aspect of a vast and piecemeal effort at having our Culture and eating it too.

All of these efforts tread a thin line. Some call it "credibility," some call it "sincerity" or "show business," and others mercifully spare us their jargon. The core of the problem, and the thing that makes the tightrope act so difficult, is that the innovator remains committed to the Culture he is precipitating and innovating against in its most essential form: that of its distinction between "the innate" and the realm of human action. For he is "doing" the innate, creating what is "natural" and uncreatable, and the Culture that he both precipitates and works against pursues him as his very (compulsive) motivation. He must work and justify himself according to the standards and demands of the thing he is working to renew. And so the advertiser tells us that he is "bringing news about better products for better living," the newscaster is "telling it like it is," the scientist gives us "fact," and the entertainer "helps people to relax." If these people want to retain credibility and legitimacy in the eyes of those for whom they create, they must convey in their acts and mannerisms the impression that they are *not* consciously contriving, that they are "playing." The scientist "explores" or "experiments," the entertainer "acts," the newscaster mocks himself in a dry way and plays on "human interest," and advertising clowns around with hokey and silly "commercials." It is a "play" that is "real," in the way that all play must be "real" if it is to be any good at all.[6]

For the alternative to "playing" at re-creating Culture is the serious fabrication of Culture, a fabrication that takes on the aspect of exploitation. When "play" tips its hand it becomes serious stuff, and when the "play" of our innovators becomes relativized, it turns into the *creation* (rather than the hypothesizing) of fact, the *fabrication* (rather than a solution) of needs, the differentiation (rather than the entertainment) of people. Serious "play" is our antidote to our relativized Culture, and if this play is relativized, we are *really* in a jam.

Consider the weather forecaster. Weather is by definition unpre-

6. Many of our theories of play regard the "phenomenon" as either disguised seriousness or an irresponsible laxity of "letting everything go." This is a familiar reduction of the problematic to absolutes that our science seems to specialize in. See Helen Beale's brilliant discussion in " 'Real Pretending': An Ethnography of Symbolic Play Communication" (Doctoral Dissertation, Department of Anthropology, Northwestern University, 1973).

dictable. It is created by our expectation of seasonal regularities: whether meteorological events do or do not occur as we expect them to, and to what degree they do or do not, is what we mean by "weather." But look what the weatherman has to do—he attempts to extend our expectation down to the minute particulars of everyday life. He *makes* the weather as much as any New Guinean tribesman does by extending the thing that defines it. And by precipitating the weather, so to speak, he often precipitates his audience—inadvertently conning them into going out without an umbrella because he said it was going to be a nice day. And even if his predictions work out splendidly, he only succeeds in convincing people that he has some kind of "inside line": they *believe* him, take him seriously, and set themselves up for even greater disappointments when his predictions finally *do* fail. And so the weatherman has to be a funny man, a kind of weather-wit; he has to goof around a lot, in a constant effort to make people *not take him seriously.*

The newscaster must "play" too, but here the self-mockery must be much more subtle, though a slightly awkward name and a certain strength of mannerism help. He must be able to flit in and out of the objective world of crisis and controversy, tempering the intensity of factual news flashes with an air of sternly personable good nature, and the frequent triviality of "human interest items" with something of his teletype objectivity. He must be consciously ambiguous in order to make his news both real and possible. And entertainers, advertisers, artists, scientists, hippies, and politicians all retain this kind of ambiguity in their styles. Our more successful presidents have been those who knew how to "play" while doing what they had to do.

Advertising rescues itself from the accusation of being too "serious," of manipulating peoples' needs and wants, by being funny. A funny commercial is a good commercial; it saves itself from the embarrassing fact that it *is* "just a commercial" by providing entertainment. (Others provide "news," or redemption.) Beneath the mask of entertaining us, or informing us, or redeeming us, the advertisement makes its small contribution to the work of creating Culture by creating its ambience, sustaining "the economy" by renewing our credibility. Together with the other facets of interpretive culture it saves us from the apathy and chaos of relativization and ambiguity at the expense of its own seriousness—it makes the distinction between the innate and the artificial a real one by reveling in its artificiality.

Thus our ostensible interaction of Culture and nature is, in fact, a dialectic of convention continually reinterpreted by invention, and invention continually precipitating convention. Even this renewal, however, is steadily losing ground, for as the effects of interpretation become more and more obvious, the essential distinction (Culture versus nature) that it precipitates undergoes greater and greater relativization. We become increasingly dependent upon interpretation, and on the enthusiasm for renewal that interrelation generates. Culture yields to Culture-cult because it has to. And if the ecologists, with their sure instinct for cutting to the bone of morality and seriousness, speak of the whole thing in terms of "life" and "survival," we should consider one thing. A polluted river or lake (pollution is Culture viewed from the standpoint of nature) teems with life. It is "survival" at its most ebullient; where a few cells once eked out a living, millions now pullulate. A bacterial "mass culture" indeed, but a "life" that no one really wants.

chapter 4

The invention of self

**An important message for you
about the makers of time**

It is generally assumed that our Culture, with its science and its technology, operates by measuring, predicting, and harnessing a world of natural "forces." But in fact the whole range of conventional controls, our "knowledge," our literatures of scientific and artistic achievement, our arsenal of productive technique, is a set of devices for the *invention* of a natural and phenomenal world. By assuming that we merely measure, predict, or harness this world of situations, individuals, and forces, we mask the fact that we create it. In our conventional belief that this measuring, predicting, and harnessing is *artificial,* part of the domain of human manipulation and inherited, cumulative "knowledge" and Culture, we precipitate this phenomenal world as a part of the innate and the inevitable. The significant aspect of this invention, its *conventional* aspect, is that its product must be taken *very seriously,* so that it is no invention at all, but *reality*. If the inventor keeps this seriousness firmly in mind (as a "safety rule," if for no other reason) while doing his job of measuring, predicting, or harnessing, then the resulting experience of "nature" will sustain his conventional distinctions. The invention of nature is serious for us for the same reason that our invention of Culture must be nonserious, or "funny."

Like so many things, our technological Culture must "fail" if it is to succeed, for its very failures constitute the thing that it is trying to measure, harness, or predict. If the formulae and predictions of science were completely effective and exhaustive, if the operations of technology were completely efficient, then nature would become science or technology itself. (This is actually how we talk about things in our modern world of contextual relativity: nature is "system," it is "biology" or "ecology," whereas Culture is "natural," an "evolutionary adaptation.") Science and technology "produce" our Cultural distinction between the innate and the artificial to the extent that they fail to be completely exact or efficient, precipitating an image of "the unknown" and of uncontrolled natural force. Thus it is that science and technology (as opposed to our "interpreted" view of them) are aligned on the side of conservatism in modern America. But it should be emphasized that even technologically our Culture "works" in terms of objectification, and *only incidentally* in terms of energy and efficiency.

Technology is the subtle art of putting together complex mechanisms upon which "natural event" impinges in such a way as to sustain their workings. Its design and efficiency depends upon our ability to *predict*. Machines are Culture, they are concrete conventional controls that simultaneously objectify the impinging phenomenal events as "Culturalized nature" (electricity, horsepower, "energy," performance), and are in turn objectified as "naturalized Culture" (machines as having capabilities, being "powerful," "intelligent," and so forth). What they produce in terms of inefficiency, friction, inertia, or "the unknown," is our palpable realization of nature as an opposing entity.

Consider the generation of "hydroelectric power." Falling water, which has been evaporated through the effects of the sun and air and been precipitated out over elevated terrain, is said to have a certain amount of "power." But if this force is not "harnessed" through human intervention, it remains a raw potential, and if it is not "computed" through the application of human techniques and measuring devices, the potential remains unknown. Whether as potential or actuality, the power must be created by selecting the appropriate Cultural measuring or converting devices for natural event to impinge upon. These devices objectify event as "power" or "energy" in one way or another.

But this invention of nature as "power" (the usable power of electricity, the "wasted" power of inertia and friction) could never take place if human beings had not already invented the cultural and technological means by which the objectification could be effected. Without the mathematics of volume and velocity or the physics of heat, gravitation, and electricity, the potential could not be calculated. Without the technology of dam building, turbines, generators, transformers, and power transmission, the potential could not be realized. All these techniques and procedures are the result of human invention, which gives characteristics to technological Culture that are transferred to nature in the course of objectifying it. We have gotten into the habit of looking at natural phenomena in terms of power potential, as *resources* (in the way that a fox looks at a goose), and are apt to forget that the real resources are those of human invention. As a part of Culture, technology is a means of storing that invention, focusing the collective creativity of many thousands of thinkers and inventors upon the tasks of objectifying nature that make up our everyday lives. The power we tap in harnessing waterfalls, combustion, or radioactive decay is that of human creativity, for without the invention of Culture that this creativity originates and embodies, Culture, in turn, could not be used to invent nature.

Technology interposes its devices in such a way that the impingement of natural event can be construed in terms of "forces" running them. Science likewise puts "system" into nature, and then delights in discovering it there; it stamps natural phenomena with a systemic form, and its theories with a natural inevitability. This is not the conventional view of these activities; we have been taught to comprehend the "natural regularities" that they precipitate as innate and eternal, as a "physical world." Nor are science and technology the only, or by any means the most subtle or pervasive, means of invention that we use. Our whole collective Culture can be seen as a set of controls ("tools," as they say) to this end, and the whole natural, phenomenal universe as the object and product of the invention. Just as the "forces" of nature run our technology and the "laws" of nature validate our theories, so natural phenomena are always created as some kind of spontaneous or motivating force.

Time, as the essence of this innate and inevitable spontaneity, is in this sense our most important product. We make time (and not only when we are "dating"). Like space, time could never be perceived without the distinctions we impose upon it. But we have fortified ourselves with a welter of temporal systems and distinctions that would make a conscientious Mayan priest dizzy. *We* create the year, academic and fiscal, and the day, whether holiday or workday, in terms of the events and situations that make them significant and worthwhile, and we do so by *predicting* them and then seeing how the events and situations impinge on our expectations. Calendars, schedules, timetables, and seasonal expectations and routines are all "predictive" devices for precipitating (and thereby surprising ourselves with, and *not predicting*) time. They are a means of setting up expectations, which in their fulfillment or nonfulfillment, become "the passage of time," "the weather," "a good time," or "a bad year." By extending our calibrations and our expectations into periods of years, decades, centuries, and even millennia, we are able to precipitate (statistically and otherwise) a temporal and often cyclical "reality." We have fiscal "boom" and "bust" periods, depressions and recessions, historical "developments," cycles, and "ages."

We know time (and its brothers "growth," "life," and "the weather") by its stealthy habit of creeping up on us. We *make it* creep up by assuming that we are able to predict and prepare for it. Our realization that our preparations and predictions have failed to some degree ("it's later than you think") amount to an experience of "the passage of time." My three-year-old daughter, learning to "tell time," summed it up well in her concise and oft-repeated expression "it's late o'clock," spoken with a grown-up urgency. "Creeping up" is an attribute our invention of the temporal and situational shares with all things that are conventionally counterinvented; the often-described "society" or "social structure" of tribal peoples "creeps up" and surprises them in much the same way. We "do" an embattled Culture, harassed and motivated by time; they do "time" as their "own thing," harassed and motivated by culture.

Inevitably, though, our objectification of time through predictive controls leads to a certain relativization. The predictive devices themselves take on a certain "natural" quality and urgency, and the individual and incidental events that they "order" assume a systematic (rhythmic) and ordered character. We speak of a "biological clock," "developmental cycles," and "the life cycle," and entertain chemical theories of maturity, sexuality, and aging that play like a bad pun upon the double meaning (biochemical and biographical) that we give to the word "life." Our "year" is full of attitudes, inclinations, disappointments, "holiday spirit," and so on, which we conventionally ascribe to its cyclical nature, to the "year" itself. We have a quickening of pace in September and October, a "holiday season," doldrums in January and February, "results" in April and May. And our day, too, with its morning and evening, our week, with its hopeless Monday, thankful Friday, and sometimes gloomy Sunday objectifies moods and attitudes in terms of cyclical "prediction." We have our "daily grind" and our "grinding holidays."

The calendar, the clock, and the schedule, in their "predictive" or organizing aspect as collectivizing controls, correspond to a deliberately

artificial and cumulative "knowledge," a morality of conventional distinction and discernment. They divide our labor from our rest, our
"serious" working life from our periods of relaxation, sleeping, eating,
and "play," and from the "holiday spirit" of compulsive individuation
in terms of gift-giving (the "generosity" that Mauss so perceptively
compared with the ordinary life of tribal peoples) and Christmas-card
writing. *We,* collectively, and often by act of Congress, manipulate
the schedules, set the "times," "plan our lives," and *it* (that mysterious
"it" or "id," the "innate" that comprehends the whole of our situational and idiosyncratic being) does the creeping, surprising—delighting
or disappointing—us, as the case may be. This, too, is what "dating"
is all about, a negotiation for "available time" (and money) that is
traditionally initiated and maintained by the male participant. The
woman (with her "natural" role, her allegedly "intuitive" identification with the rhythmic and the innate) is in charge of surprises.

What we mean by "time," and the thing that stands behind this
whole landscape of cycles, the situational, the innately human, the
movement and evolution of "natural force" and the phenomenal
world, is the inventive dialectic—the contradictory, paradoxical, and
moving aspect of culture. Our Culture of purposive prediction and
knowledge-gathering precipitates this dialectical movement by counterinventing it, and because of the inevitable masking that occludes this
form of objectification, we decline to take responsibility for it. We say
that it is innate in us, that it "is" us, that it is "reality," mapped into
the rhythms of nature and the urgency of our phenomenal world. It
underlies and grounds our deep and peculiar fear of mortality, the
sickness and death that we also precipitate in many ways. We do not
"do" it, but only "play" at it, or perceive it, to the point where our
very notions of "invention," "play," and "metaphor" are relegated to
the catch-all of the "merely symbolic."

Our Culture is a life style that has elected to draw its conventional
distinctions deliberately and consciously, rather than to precipitate
them. This is what we mean by "rules," a morality of deliberate and
artificial articulation. And because we "do" convention, we must "be"
and suffer the exigencies of invention, its dialectical antithesis. Invention is our surprise, our mystery, our natural necessity. It is the reflex,
the "other side," but also the "cause" and the motivation of our conscious action. Thus the control (and masking) of invention is a *moral
duty* for us, something that we *should do* if we are to live and preserve our mysteries. It is the morality of knowledge, or science, and
of a government that feels the need to build society, and develop and
improve the lot of mankind.

Whenever we invoke and participate in this morality, whether as citizens by voting and "showing concern"; as technicians, by operating and building machines; or as scientists, by creating "knowledge" and formulating definitions, we subtly and inadvertently create its motivating mystery. We create, and propel ourselves with, our problems as we go. Public trust creates corruption (in the form of well-meaning politicians who want to keep a controlling hand on "the dirty world of political reality" for good causes), integration creates "minorities," machines manufacture "natural force," and definition precipitates the indefinable. Moreover, our controls in this action, our knowledge, our science, our machinery of government and government of machinery are *our responsibility.* The more they become relativized into a Culture that "works by itself" and a nature that needs conscious intervention if it is to "work" at all, the greater the felt *moral need* for reform, for restoring the conventional distinction between the innate and the artificial. We may feel this need as a necessity to oppose fascism, to decry automation, to "return" to nature, to conserve our resources or preserve the Environment, but we cannot avoid it. Of course the more we respond to it by affording the government greater autonomy in the name of the people to conserve and remake nature, the more we relativize our distinction. Fascism always comes to power "in the name of the people."

It is not only such obviously collective and "made" conventions as government and knowledge that embody our moral world. Everything we "make" participates in it. There is a morality of "things," of objects in their conventional meanings and conventional uses. Even tools are not so much purely "functional" utilitarian devices as a kind of common human or Cultural property, heirlooms that constrain their users in learning to use them. We might even suggest, like the poet Rainer Maria Rilke, that tools "use" human beings, toys "play with" children, weapons lure us to battle. Speaking of the things known in childhood, Rilke noted:

> This Something, worthless at is was, prepared your relationships with the world, it guided you into happening and among people, and, further: you experienced through it, through its existence, through its anyhow-appearance, through its final smashing or its enigmatic departure, all that is human, right into the depths of death.[1]

In our living with these toys, tools, articles, and heirlooms, desiring them, treasuring them, we admit into our personalities the whole

1. Rainer Maria Rilke, *Gesammelte Werke,* IV, 377–78, in *Duino Elegies,* tr. with introduction and commentary by J. B. Leishman and Stephen Spender (New York: W. W. Norton, 1939), p. 100.

range of values, attitudes, and sentiments—indeed the creativity—of those who invented them, used them, know and desire them, or gave them to us. In learning to use tools we are secretly learning to use ourselves; as controls the tools merely mediate the relation, they objectify our skills. The same is true of our "materialistic" longings and pleasures.

The objects and other human phenomena that surround us, and indeed all things that have a cultural significance or value, are "invested" with life in this respect; they partake of the self, and also create it. "Mass production" and its commercial and technological concomitants can only, in the light of this fact, lead to a kind of inflation of human character and qualities. We have disposable emotions, ideas that expend their energies in "nine-day-wonder" orgies of fast living, literatures whose editions experience insectlike cycles of nuptial flight, hibernation, reemergence, metamorphosis, and so on, and finally, alas, disposable people.

And those ultimate artifacts, our cities, are likewise controls for the precipitation of "life," of a social and Cultural life that cannot be produced without their order and ambience. They are what Culture has accumulated to, and indispensable to the "selves" and cycles, the "feelings," that depend on that order. And so, in a highly relativized world, they become a "natural" habitat, environment as well as order. The city is Culture, and becomes as ambiguous as Culture itself; it is a context (every city is a context, right out to the city limits) that was and is articulated deliberately, precipitating a necessity that becomes the very necessity of civilization. It is the greatest of our "double binds" (all relativized contexts are double binds, this is why and how they frustrate), at once the solution and the container of our problems. Vast, crumbling collectivities of mortar, asphalt, steel, and knowledge, our cities teem with the "protest individuation" of crime and sarcasm (often relativized to the point of being organized crime and politicized sarcasm). Like the economic and commercial Culture ("money") that forms its lifeblood, and is sustained by the inventive motivation of advertising, the city is Culture in spite of itself: watch Culture parody itself in the piling up of skylines and of slums. Even those who flee it carry the ambiguity with them into the suburban accretions they build around it as a city beyond the city, a city in spite of itself.

Yet Culture in spite of itself is still Culture; however much it is relativized it builds outward and upward by clinging to its convention of collective enterprise and the innateness of nature; it does so *in order to cling to this convention*. But the very fact of relativization, of ambiguous controls that do not "work" as they should, underlines most clearly that the creative opposite of Culture is *not* the image of "nature" and Environment that haunts us like a ghost of virgin forests and pristine streams. Nature, alas, is "system" in spite of itself, and ambiguous as Culture. By addressing ourselves to a relativized nature we *obviate* Culture, and vice versa. The collective articulation of conventional distinctions that is knowledge and Culture must always operate in a dialectic with individuation and invention if it is to operate at all, and so it must precipitate individuation and invention as its motivation and mystery. It is to this invention, in its most personal and individual form, that we shall now turn.

Learning personality

We do not normally think of the self as a product of human action, especially of its own action. Something, that is to say, must represent a kind of "input," a "given" beyond all the "influences" of education and socialization that impinges upon and affects Culture. Yet if we accept this assumption in its orthodox, "everyday" sense, we deny the whole significance of our discussion of invention. For the door will be left open to those who tell us that man is ultimately motivated by natural impulses, such as "instincts," "drives," and a "need for gratification." And even if we reject the assumption, remembering how easily "needs" are created in advertising, and decide that a person's motivations are largely determined by social influences and education, we will by-pass the significance of invention. For the popular cliché that "the individual is a product of his society" makes man into a social rather than a natural automaton. Our only alternative is to regard *the individual's own actions* as the significant "input" in determining the self. And this emphasis on invention brings the matter of convention into play.

First and foremost, the thing that anchors every actor to his world of dialectical invention is his commitment to a convention that identifies one mode of objectification as pertaining to his "innate" self, and the other with external and impinging actions. Since this convention can only be sustained and carried forward by acts of invention, and since invention can only result in effective and meaningful expression when subject to the orientation of convention, neither can be regarded as a determinant. Both are equally involved in, and equally products of, the successive acts of combining and distinguishing cultural contexts that constitute man's social and individual life. When an actor's commitment to some particular identification of a cultural "self" becomes ambiguous and relativized to a significant extent, he is trapped in a cyclical maelstrom of indeterminate intentions, a neurosis or hysteria of "personal" and "external" commitments drawing upon and "using" one another. The predicament is that of invention out of relation to convention, and the cure is a matter of bringing these into alignment by developing a controlled and manageable relation between them.

We create the self out of the world of action, and the world of action out of the self. Since both these realms—whichever we take to be the domain of convention—are equally products of dialectical invention, neither can be positively described as the source of our personal and emotional difficulties. The crises and tribulations of the individual "psyche" are experienced and created (and hence "masked") through conceptions of innate "drives" and motivations and external compulsions or "guiding spirits," the products of the actor's commitment to a particular conventional orientation. Self and spirit, id, ego, and superego are cultural illusions born of a particular cultural viewpoint; the real problem is that of *the relation between them*. The formation and management of this relation is thus the crucial factor in the development of the individual. It is a struggle against the relativization of convention that amounts to neurosis or hysteria, and its "losers" are not the victims of demonic internal or external forces ("natural cravings," "society," a "possessed soul") but of a defeating inventive orientation that sets personal efforts against themselves. For all peoples, the creation of an effective relation implies gaining a certain expertise in manipulating the "innate"; for "creative" individuals, this leads to an inversion of the conventional identification of what one "is" versus what one "does." For modern American ideology, given its identification of particularizing objectification with the "innate," this is a problem of managing invention—of what we call the "personality."

"Personality" is the concern of the Culture of the urban middle class, which Schneider has described and analyzed in his studies of American kinship, and which he distinguishes from the interpretive worlds of upper- and lower-class kinship.[2] Culture provides a common set of symbolic and actional forms for all Americans, over and above those of their particular (class, "ethnic," or individual) orientations, and sustains the framework of public life, of law courts, schools, production, and administration. Those who participate in the mainstream of our civilization, the "white-collar workers," commercial and pro-

2. David M. Schneider and Raymond T. Smith, *Class Differences and Sex Roles in American Kinship and Family Structure* (Englewood Cliffs, N.J.: Prentice-Hall, 1973).

fessional classes and their families, who subscribe to the reality of
nature and the importance of science and a good education, build
their lives through it and objectify their actions in terms of its controls. Others, the "ethnic" and "religious" lower classes, the dissatis-
fied and disenfranchised, the "creative" upper classes, must come to
terms with it through dialectical confrontation—something that takes
a bewildering variety of forms, from the "interpretation" of advertising, government, entertainment, and protest, to "exploitation" and
crime.

The "self" precipitated by this Culture (Freud's "id") is individual,
particularistic, and nevertheless spontaneous and motivating. It is
experienced as a seemingly "internal" and personal aspect of the
natural world, as an amalgam of natural forces, drives, and urges.
Generally identified with the form and workings of man's "physical"
makeup, with hormones, chemistry, and cognition, it is in fact invention disguised as "life." The "self" grows, it "creeps up" like time and
the weather, and is often represented in cyclical terms—bodily
"rhythms," female periods and sensitivities. Like time, situation, and
the weather, it is created by consciously articulating the conventional
controls of Culture, by attempting to predict, control, and constrain
it. "Self" comes into being as the motivating "resistance" to these attempts. For instance, sexual "drives" are not only directed or chan-
neled, but actually *invented* through our attempts to anticipate and
control them; the naughtiness of a naughty child is brought into being
by our expectations and sanctions in disciplining him. Indeed, all our
training and educational procedures, our theories of "child development" and the expectations they bring about, are simply "masks" for
the collective invention of a "natural" self. This invention is by no
means limited to childhood or education; the schedules, occupations,
and programs for human performance that constitute our collective
Culture are a vast assemblage of controls for the creation of the
natural self. The artist or writer precipitates a motivating "talent,"
the artisan or administrator creates his "skills," the scientist or engi-
neer invents his "ingenuity," and even the taker of an intelligence
"test" uses its forms to produce an impression of his "native intelligence."

Invention, as the "natural self," is internal and mysterious for us
precisely because we regard convention, in the form of collective Culture, as artificial and external. The more we strive to use and develop
cultural artifices—theories, technologies, programs for action—in an
effort to decipher the mystery and control and apply its properties, the
more soundly and surely we invent its innateness and its mysteries.
The phenomenal world will always elude the physicist (as Heisenberg

showed us), cognition will forever evade the dedicated ethnoscientist, and the ingenious naughtiness of children will perpetually evade the disciplines and moralizing programs of their "developers." Participation in an artificial Culture of collective enterprise precipitates invention as its antithesis.

But we have learned that invention must continually "invert" itself in the interest of preserving convention. So the very motivational constitution of the middle-class American obliges him to "use," to deliberately and consciously articulate his innate and individual "self" from time to time in the course of his activities. When we use the image of the individual self in this way, as a differentiating control, we call it the "personality" (Freud's "ego"). It is conscious invention, what the artist, researcher, entertainer, and advertiser make a profession of, and also the difficult and often frustrating kind of objectification that we intend when we attempt to "be ourselves." As a differentiating role, the personality precipitates a collectivizing motivation (Freud's "superego"), a counterinvention of conventional moral order in the form of a compulsive "conscience." The personality is an acting "self," a deliberate individuality prompted by and motivated through a precipitated Culture. The motivating "resistance" experienced and created in this manner, by the ways in which one's actions fail to conform to the image of the control, takes the form of *guilt*. Guilt is the critique of "personality."

All the "creative," "recreational," and restorative activities of middle-class Americans, all the things they do to renew, refresh, and reevaluate their lives, are pursued by a guilty motivation. We eat, smoke, brush our teeth, clean house, and vacation compulsively, hounded by the dire alternatives of one kind of excess or another—malnutrition versus overeating; germs, dirt, and unhealthiness versus wasted and meaningless ritual; nervous tension versus the fear of cancer or of wasting time. The personality precipitates and responds to convention in its most essential form, the distinction between the innate and the artificial. Guilt is ultimately an *awareness* of inappropriate (i.e., "relativizing") invention (as shame, its opposite, is a *demonstration* of inappropriate awareness); we feel guilt as a result of transgressing the moral distinction between what we *are* and what we *do*, manipulating the former and neglecting the latter.

Just as the phenomenon of motivation is by no means "internal," but extends outward into the people and things that surround us, so the inversion by which we become aware of personality is subject to the manipulation of interpersonal relationships. We make each other *feel guilty* by projecting this awareness, adopting the role of Cultural conscience and forcing others into a consciousness of their inventive selves. Guilt motivates the redress of a conventional imbalance, and there are formal and informal social roles, and even whole industries (advertising and government no less than organized charities) founded on the simple device of redefining convention in such a way as to make people feel guilty. It is the mainstay of our cult-life (official as well as unofficial), and therefore, indirectly, of our Culture. But it is also practically an institutionalized neurosis.

The trick of learning personality is that of learning not to take oneself (one's personality) seriously, of mastering the technique of creating and responding to guilt (in ourselves and in others) in such a way that the conventional distinction between what one is and what one does is maintained. It is the art of invention in a world whose serious business is the articulation of convention; like advertising, weather-forecasting, entertainment, and the other aspects of interpretive culture, it must "play" and sacrifice its own seriousness in order that convention (Culture) may be taken seriously. A healthy, effective personality is one that keeps its sense of "self" unambiguous and clear-cut by making its manipulation of individuality hypothetical, tentative, and "funny"; in so doing it precipitates a sharply defined conventional distinction. A personality that takes itself too seriously, on the other hand, plays at convention; it counterfeits Culture and cultural convention, manufacturing guilt as a means to action. This is what we mean by obsessional or compulsive neurosis: neurotic "rituals" allow the individual to act successfully (to manipulate the self very seriously) by precipitating a motivating and justifying but highly idiosyncratic "convention."

Learning personality is always a flirtation with neurosis, because it is very difficult both to "do" or manipulate the self as a differentiating control and to not take this control seriously. The temptation, and the inclination, is always to do a good job of making the self over into a preferred image, and thus to precipitate conventions that will justify (and indeed motivate) the action. This is the problem of children, of adolescents, and especially of adults who wish to be professionally creative. The whole of the actor's universe can only be sustained, experienced, and dealt with through continual *invention*, but since invention can only sustain its orientation and its meaningful communication by precipitating the right kind of *convention*, the actor in modern Western culture must learn to project and experience his personality as spontaneous and innate. He can "play" with it, discipline it, or seek out channels for its enrichment or growth, but he can only take ultimate responsibility for what he "is" at the cost of precipitating a private world of neurotic compulsion. He must learn to invent his personality, his invention, as innate.

Precisely because we learn by doing, and because this kind of "doing" is difficult to master, neurosis is a common experience for all of us. Learning to control it is learning to invent the world right; it is learning "a sense of responsibility." It is particularly those who are learning to "deal with" (to create) the world from a new standpoint— a child, an adult, as a creator or administrator—who face the problem of learning to invent a conventional "responsibility." (The Freudian "latency period" is simply the quietude of a child who has learned to act as a child, to recognize his play *as* "play.") The beginnings of this can be seen early in a child's life. In attempting things she had been severely warned against (sometimes with punishment), my twenty-two-month-old daughter would attack the matter with great zeal, muttering "no no no no" under her breath. Right or wrong, an invention is an invention and carries its own motivation. But the example illustrates very clearly the way in which discipline can produce a realization of convention. One could not really argue that she did not know the proper meaning of the negative, since she used it with perfect accuracy. She was learning (by doing) to perceive the negation of "correct" action as an impulse. And yet this impulse, the "no no no no," remained entirely encompassed within her world of play; when I reversed roles and pretended to be her "baby," the only thing I could do to induce her to spank me was to start crying.

The priority of invention (and hence the tendency to neurosis) in a child's learning of personality is strikingly illustrated in the creation of "imaginary playmates" by small children. These are actually modes of interpretation through the invention of artificial social orders— playmates whose reported adventures, requirements, opinions, and misdemeanors motivate and excuse the child's intentions and actions. Besides his more orthodox and sociable "friends" Possum, Fran, Wiper, and Farkel, my two-and-a-half-year-old nephew was beset by a nemesis named Goppy. Goppy was continually spilling, breaking, and over-turning things, for which the poor little fellow took the blame, and in addition would insidiously fill the child's diaper once or twice a day. The child's own "self," which is after all being "made" through these characterizations, may slip in and out of their roles; my daughter's friends Getty, Jamil, Jealous (who appeared shortly after the birth of her little brother), and Widing Hood would frequently do things for her that she did not want to do, and Widing Hood was only added to the pantheon after she herself had ceased to assume this role regularly.

Doubtless these creations arise in part from the child's (quite per-ceptive) observation and emulation of adults, for they follow all the "rules" by which adults manifest and excuse their acts and inclinations through gossip and anecdote about others. They appear transparent and "playful" (and, to some, trifling) because they treat rather cavalierly those patents of legitimacy that sustain and certify the inventions of adults, though to be sure such legitimation is seldom overt in conversation. In fact they represent an adaptation of conventional order to the child's own invention of self, a play world that allows him to be the kind of self he wants to be in the face of encroaching "responsibility." Though they may dissolve, proliferate, or undergo transformation, play worlds as a general phenomenon are never outgrown; people just learn to make them more convincing, tailoring their inventions to the requirements of conventional responsibility.

The world of the adolescent, of the young person learning to create adult desires and needs, presents a similar dilemma. It is necessary to make the requisite "mistakes," to invent a self very seriously in the form of wants, desires, and aspirations—thus precipitating obsessive spasms of "falling in love" and "hero worship"—if one is to develop the kind of creativity that can be shaped into a more or less conventional personality. What is a so-called "healthy" or "normal" personality but a former neurosis, a counterfeiting of Culture, that has been tempered into a rapport with convention?

Learning not to take the personality seriously means learning to take what one "should do," Cultural convention and the guilt that accompanies it, very seriously. It amounts to learning to *do* morality when one is *being* a self, and learning to *be* morality (to "be good") when one is *doing* the self. This makes the dilemma of the person who is learning to be creative in relation to his society, to deliberately and consciously objectify the innate so as to precipitate a novel and provocative image of the conventional, the most difficult dilemma of all. Like the child and the adolescent, the creative person must create and then temper his neurotic symptoms. But unlike the child and the adolescent, who must learn to "do" personality and yet not take this doing seriously, in the interests of "responsibility," he must recover from his neuroses in such a way that he is able to manipulate his personality and invention very seriously without appearing to do so, and pay his respects to the conventions of "responsibility" while living in a creative world of his own conventions. His very creativity, his ability to impinge upon the conventional world, depends on this.

Thus the creative individual is placed in a kind of "double bind." Instead of rectifying the neurotic imbalance between invention and convention by bringing it into alignment with the conventional distinction between the innate and the artificial, he must learn a personal *inversion* of this convention, *while not appearing to do so.* He must carry his neurosis "all the way," to the point of living in his own world, and use the very articulation of personality and invention by which this world is precipitated as a "bridge," to build the relation between his own world and that of cultural convention. Personality, then, is the most serious thing in the world for him, and yet he must deprecate it and reduce it to the dimensions of the nonserious if he is to maintain credibility in dealing with others. By the same token the realm of conventional "responsibility" will often seem quizzical and arbitrary to him (think of Beethoven!), for his inventive personality is motivated by a very different set of conventions; yet he *must* address his creative efforts to this larger Culture if they are to be meaningful and effective for others.

The creative personality treads a thin line between the "credibility" that links it to the everyday world of responsible convention and the motivation of its own creative impulses. One is always tempted to yield to the latter and slip into a conventional world of one's own devising, at the risk of losing "credibility" and being judged insane. Indeed, one of the great risks of the conventional inversion a creative person must undergo is losing the desire or the ability to "relate" and maintain credibility and thus becoming schizophrenic. Bateson has argued brilliantly that the schizophrenic is someone who has learned, under the impress of family conditions, to *avoid* this kind of communication:

> Typically the schizophrenic will eliminate from his message everything that refers explicitly or implicitly to the relationship between himself and the person he is addressing. Schizophrenics commonly avoid the first and second person pronouns. They avoid telling you what sort of message they are transmitting. . . .[3]

A schizophrenic, in other words, has lost or considers unimportant those points of contact that translate his statements and ideas into viable cultural meaning and power. He has learned to create the world without inventing the self, and without the help of others.

This was ultimately the refuge of Nietzsche, who at the very onset of his insanity wrote to Jacob Burckhardt, his former colleague at Basel:

> In the end I would much rather be a Basel professor than God; but I have not dared push my private egoism so far as to desist for its sake from the creation of the world.[4]

It characterizes with typically Nietzschian lucidity the plight of someone who wishes to "create the world" without the hindrance of self

3. Gregory Bateson, *Steps to an Ecology of Mind* (New York: Chandler Publishing, 1972), p. 235.
4. Friedrich W. Nietzsche, *The Portable Nietzsche,* ed. and tr. Walter Kaufmann (New York: Viking, 1954, p. 685.

or others. Whatever the "cause" of Nietzsche's insanity (there are many theories), his intellectual reaction to it is singularly appropriate for someone who had striven with great brilliance but indecisive effect to convey an idea of the "transvaluation of all values."

Nietzsche's insanity had to do with becoming serious, an unhappy consummation for the author of *The Gay Science,* who savored so well the art of playing with one's image of self, one's personality. There is a facility, a droll or grotesquely "unserious" projection of self in mockery of convention, that occurs again and again in the lives of the greatest creators. In allowing the creative personality to seemingly mock itself (not "take itself seriously"), while in fact mocking convention, it serves as a viable and cathartic "solution" to the creative double-bind. Beethoven, a gruff master of this sort of thing, wrote his Diabelli Variations as a joke, and Rembrandt depicted the hero of *Samson Threatening His Father-in-Law* as himself, and also included himself among the soldiers engaged in crucifying Christ (*The Raising of the Cross*). But the masterpiece of this kind of playful mockery is by Jan Vermeer, of whom one commentator remarked that "there are signs in him of an immense disdain." [5] In *The Painter's Art* (now called *An Artist in His Studio* or *The Allegory of Fame*), the artist (quite likely Vermeer himself) has his *back* to the viewer, and one sees only his model, a rather giddy "muse of history" holding a book and a trombone-like instrument in a ridiculous and self-conscious pose. Here is the "anonymous artist," caught in his all-too-serious act of capturing "Fame" on the canvas, but also a "Fame" who is herself "made up" and self-conscious!

The anthropologist too, in his manipulation of personality to accord with the expectations of some unfamiliar way of life—precipitating that life style as a personal "convention," undergoes a creative inversion. Whether or not he uses this strategic role, this creation of self as intellectual relation, to mock his own conventions (and the temptation is very great, in a relativized Culture, to do so), his situation makes the issue of comparative conventions a pressing one. He sees this issue as the problem of Culture, but is it *always* this?

On "doing your own thing": The world of immanent humanity

Whether we call it time, growth, invention, personality, or, in the shorthand of modern mass culture, "change," we precipitate the incidental and the inventive (or evolutionary) aspect of things as our

5. Lawrence Gowing, *Jan Vermeer* (New York: Barnes & Noble, 1962), p. 73.

great motivating mystery. Consciously and purposefully we "do" the distinction between what is innate and what is artificial by articulating the controls of a conventional, collective Culture. But what of those peoples who conventionally "do" the particular and the incidental, whose lives seem to be a kind of continual improvization? Can we understand them in terms of something that we "do" and they do not deliberately strive to achieve? By making invention, and hence time, growth, and change a part of their deliberate "doing," they precipitate something analogous to our Culture, but do not and cannot conceive of it as Culture. It is not artifice, but the universe. The conventional, be it grammar, kin relations, social order ("norm" and "rule"), is for them an innate, motivating, and "creeping" (thus unaccountable) distinction between what is innate and what is artificial. This "knowledge," as we call it, cannot be for them a subject of "learning" and discussion in our conventional sense; rather it partakes of the immanent essence of all things, accessible only to the greatest seers and shamans, and compelled and precipitated as a brilliant flash of insight in the course of divination, religious inspiration, and introspection.

A phenomenal world manifesting an implicit human social and conventional order is an anthropomorphic one. Behind every phenomenal event, be it part of human sociality or of the surrounding living and nonliving environment, lurks the enigmatic possibility of an anthropomorphic or sociomorphic explanation. There is a conventional certainty, in other words, that the ultimate causality of things is constituted in terms of one's particular (and necessarily innate) conventional order. The conceptions themselves may be explicit, such as named deities considered "forces" or predispositions of the universe, or a "creation" like the mythically potent landscape of the Australian aborigines; or they may be diffuse, like the Daribi notion that the movements of the sun and the water prefigure the course of human mortality. Again, the anthropomorphism may take on a different form and a different significance under the impress of various ceremonial, mythological, and divinatory procedures for compelling and discovering the innate. But whatever the form his machinations give it, this immanent humanity presents man with the continual urgency of controlling, compelling, and ascertaining its nature. As the "order" of things and of people, it is not "power" in the sense of our natural world (though it manifests itself through power), but rather the key to power, the knowledge that bestows power and that power can help one to win.

If Americans and other Westerners create the incidental world by constantly trying to predict, rationalize, and order it, then tribal, religious, and peasant peoples create their universe of innate convention by constantly trying to change, readjust, and impinge upon it. Our

concern is that of bringing things into an ordered and consistent relation—whether one of logically organized "knowledge" or practically
organized "application"—and we call the summation of our efforts
Culture. Their concern might be thought of as an effort to "knock
the conventional off balance," and so make themselves powerful and
unique in relation to it. If we understand "power" to represent invention, an individual force or element that impinges upon the collectivities of society, then the urban Westerner "is" power (in the sense
of his "innate" individuality and special gifts and talents) and "does"
morality (his "performance"), whereas the religious or tribal person
"does" or "follows" power (special roles, guiding magic, or spiritual
helpers) and "is" moral.

The conventionally prescribed tasks of everyday life, what one
"should" do in such a society, are guided by a vast, continually changing and constantly augmented set of differentiating controls, all held
together and "cued in" by the conventional "society" that their use
precipitates. These include all manner of kin and productive roles,
magical and practical techniques, possible modes of conduct for personal deportment. And if the ethnographer finds it difficult to stan-
dardize these controls, or catch a "native" in the act of explicitly
"performing" one of them, it is because their very nature and intent
defies the kind of literalness that "standardization" or "performance"
(as well as the ethnographer's own professional ethic of consistency)
implies. They are *not* Culture, they are not intended to be "performed"
or followed as a "code," *but rather used as the basis of inventive
improvisation.* The trick of using them is a matter of exaggeration and
improvising, and it can and often does involve a certain degree of
mockery or buffoonery. The person who is able to do this well—even
to the point of inventing wholly new controls—is admired and often
emulated. The controls are themes to be "played upon" and varied,
rather in the way that jazz lives in a constant improvisation of its
subject matter.

And so we can speak of this form of action as a continual adventure
in "unpredicting" the world. By trying consciously and deliberately to
assert his uniqueness and independence of others, the actor invariably
fails to some degree, betraying inadvertently his essential "humanity"
and similarity to others. And this failure, as a counterinvention of the
very conventional world he is trying to "unpredict," serves as his
motivation. It amounts to the subliminal and unintended mode of
objectification, the collectivization of his differentiating control—a
creeping invention of the social and moral order *in spite of* his intentions. As the very opposite of our invention of "nature" through the

consistencies of machinery, schedules, books, and reasons, this enterprise is bound to be both unfamiliar and provocative to us.

These people live *through* their cults and enthusiasms almost exclusively, so that life is a succession of highly charged expectations and adventures. It is "metaphorical" and paradoxical, a commitment to something for the sake of something else, and therefore its essential intent and impact is utterly lost if taken literally. The course of life is something like our advertising, constantly "redeeming" society by living it through some kind of novel or magical control. The ordinary imageries it follows, its "powers" (like the power of "bushfowl magic" in gardening) are and must be wild slogans, ideals to be believed in (for this is what makes them "work") but scarcely taken literally. By taking them too explicitly or too literally we confuse them with the ends to which they are addressed, the exact "knowledge" and conventional order that constitute the nature of things. So there can be many "kinds" of magic, many alternative "roles" or procedures, many "roads to knowledge," whose measure of acceptance and usefulness is not their literal content, but whether they "work" (that is, whether one can believe in them). Among the Daribi, whose personal names share this differentiating aspect, many people bear names like *merawai* ("filth-spoken," "filthy") and *dinabo* ("eats excrement"), which no one regards as pejorative.

Life as inventive sequence has a particular character, a certain quality of brilliance that beggars comparison with our busy busy world of responsibility and performance. It is *this*, not "nutrition" or "survival," that animated the long-gone camps that our archeologists study as charcoal diagrams; it is *this*, not "primitiveness" or "stone-age mentality," that makes the contradictory and paradoxical encounters of "middle-class" people with peasants, tribal peoples, and those of the "lower class," and it is this that is "missing" in a camp or village denuded of its population by labor-recruiting and so on. The dullness that we find in mission schools, refugee camps, and sometimes in "acculturated" villages is symptomatic not of the absence of "Culture," but of the absence of its very antithesis—that "magic," that very swaggering image of boldness and invention that *makes* culture, precipitating its regularities by failing in some final sense to overcome them.

The nonliteral nature of differentiating controls allows them to be understood, to some extent, as indirect and "tricky" procedures, though this awareness never reaches the point of admitting that the trickery *creates* the innate. The innate properties of things are tricked, compelled, cajoled, elicited (just as our "innate" temporality and natural "forces" are predicted, understood, or applied) by human action, but not brought into being by that action. It is the given order of things that is tricked, not the actor himself. The realization that one is tricking oneself would obviate the act, it would "unmask" the transformation that the actor believes himself to be effecting. The differentiating controls, whether in fact they approximate our notion of "magic," or have to do with "technology" or "kinship" or the influence of a guiding "power" or saint, are prized as ingenious devices for the coercion of the "given" order of things on one's behalf. Thus Daribi explained the operation of their spells to me in terms of deliberate "trickery," cajoling and conjuring the intended result. But the bushfowl's garden-clearing ability was "tapped" or compelled by the spell, not simply created. (If people were able to create it, the Daribi would have pointed out, then the bushfowl—and the mention of the bushfowl—would not have been necessary.)

The thought that "magical" operations *create* the innate is antithetical to the successful undertaking of the magic (though it is central to my analysis of how people create their realities); it is no more acceptable to the user of the magic than the proposition that we create natural force would be to our engineers and technicians. Rain, death, fertility, and the other objects of a sorcerer or magician are no less "innate" for the fact that they are conceived and elicited anthropomorphically. Magic does not and cannot create them, but only "help" or compel them. Thus, although we can understand mourning laments as controls *for the creation of sorrow as a conventional social state,* the native must see them as devices to help channel the expression of an innately occurring feeling; although we can analyze the Lord's Prayer as a device to create an experience of divinity, the believer must accept it as a helpful guide for the innate tendencies of his soul.

The interpretive modalities of individual action all lead to the creation of seemingly "innate" conventional states and relationships by "setting them up," "responding" to them in advance, so to speak, acting so as to elicit the response of others *and* thus make the state or response a socially de facto one. Yet, since the state or relationship is understood as an innately occurring thing, a motivating occurrence, the action is never seen or conceptualized in this way by the participants. To them it is "given"; and therefore prior; it merely begins to actualize itself—as a tendency of his soul—in the motivations of the one who initiates it. The state or relation is *there;* it is simply "recognized" with an appropriate response by the actor who initiates it. The Village Councillor at Lake Tebera "recognized" a namesake relationship between myself and his light-skinned child when I allowed the infant to pull my hair and especially when I enquired after its name; he did not mention it at the time, but when mother and child returned that afternoon by canoe, he simply announced that "your namesake is coming."

The quality of the innate among tribal, religious, and peasant peoples is a motivating discernment, an implicit conventionality or sociality (set of relationships) that seemingly "selects" its own precipitation. It is precipitated or elicited through the deliberate (inventive or improvisatory) articulation of differentiating controls. The necessities that this mode of action presents to the actor, that of "helping" or compelling the powers to work for one, of recognizing and making explicit and/or averting covert states and relationships, of pulling others into a relationship by teasing them or "putting them on their mettle," are masks for for actual *creation* of the social and the conventional. Consider the "joking" and "avoidance" relationships of tribal people the world over, that have so caught the fancy of ethnographers. The people themselves say that they "must" act in a teasing or respectful or totally anonymous way toward certain others *because* they related to the latter in a certain way. The relationship, in other words, is prior. But in fact their action in the prescribed manner *makes* the relationship, relates the people in the appropriate way. "Joking" relationships require the burlesquing of certain "inappropriate" (i.e., sexual or aggressive) behaviors on the part of one or both of the participants. As long as the participants "take it as a joke," recognizing implicitly the inappropriateness of the behavior (and hence the appropriateness of their relationship), they actually create the relationship itself as the context of their interaction. "Respect" likewise entails the avoidance of certain subjects and ways of acting; as long as both participants conspire to maintain this avoidance, and hence the appropriateness of this mode of interaction, they put themselves "in the relationship"; they create it. Nor is the situation any different for those whose relations require partial or complete avoidance; they make the appropriateness of their relationship by not having to do with one another under certain circumstances, or not having to do with one another at all.

These "styles" of familial and kin interaction differ from those of middle-class Americans in that they make family and relationship the invisible context of explicit individual action, rather than make the individual the implicit context of purposeful familial existence. The family (and for that matter "society" as a whole) is not "planned," it is precipitated. Nowhere is this more apparent than in sexual differentiation. Men and women create their interaction as such by acting *against* one another, playing "man" to someone else's "woman" and eliciting a response, putting the other sex "on its mettle," taking the meanings of masculinity and transforming them into femininity, or vice versa.

The fact that men and women in tribal, peasant, and "lower-class" groups keep to themselves, develop clubs and life styles of their own, and interact only in fighting, banter, and sexual relations is not a peripheral "psychological" problem to be explained away by theories of biology, function, or deprivation. It is central to their modality of creating social reality—it is the *means* by which this reality is created. Each sex *differentiates* itself from the other, in inventive, improvisatory, and often simply peculiar ways. By implicitly recognizing the character and qualities of the other, taunting it into being, as it were, it creates the sexual complementarity on which social life is based.

The "reciprocity" that has proven so popular in recent investigations of tribal peoples provides yet another example of explicit invention. The wealth of these societies amounts to *differentiating* value over and above its collectivizing aspect. Such wealth is not "money" because its significance as "gift"—as something in itself—always preponderates over its exchange value. One does not "buy" women and children in social exchanges, one "gives" and "receives," at best one "substitutes." The collective valuation is *elicited* by giving much or little, what is precious or what is disdained, as the case may be. One creates the appropriateness of the relationship between giver and receiver, and does so by "recognizing" its immanence. But one *does not* create the relationship per se by appeal to explicit value, and this is what distinguishes gift from money, tribal "reciprocity" from a mercantile economy. *As a matter of moral principle,* the giving of gifts is not "economic," and the elicitation of kin relationships is not "kinship."

Differentiation both precipitates the collective and is motivated by it. And this collective includes the whole common understanding of man's social life, identified as an innate tendency in man and the surrounding universe. If the urgency of a collectivizing tradition is that of controlling an overly incidental universe by rationalizing and rendering knowledgeable, then that of a differentiating tradition is the pressing and often terrible necessity of avoiding an adverse collectivization—an undesirable state, a common doom. This is what is meant by "salvation of the soul," and intended by the divination of fearful influences hanging over a community.

The problem is one of relativization, of ambiguous differentiating controls that inadvertently collectivize in ways that one did not intend. It comes about through a failure to distinguish adequately between the realms of human action and the innate, a failure that, like this distinction itself, is often a "creeping" one. In the eyes of tribal and religious peoples, it amounts to the problem of profanation and sin. The mourning practices of many tribal peoples are intended to invoke and universalize the sorrow of individual death. They "invent" the death *as* death, so to speak. But the necessity under which they labor is of *differentiating* the dead from the living, inventing death explicitly so that it is not counterinvented implicitly *as their own existential state.* ("If we did not mourn, we might see the ghosts" say the Daribi. But they also say that only the dead can see each other.) Among the Daribi the death of someone who goes unmourned (a death that is not differentiated as such) stands a chance of becoming generalized and "creeping up" in the objectified form of an outbreak of deaths, especially of children. (The ghost, to put it in native terms, has not been placed in an appropriate relationship to the living; it is angry wth them.) When this happens the living are obliged to take collective action: they differentiate *themselves* into "house people" and *habudidi,* "escorts" for the ghost, and undertake a rite of inclusion, "bringing the ghost to the house," after which, mollified, it departs for the land of the dead.

The ghost is an individualized and particular spirit-being, a part of the innate, whose relation to the living is controlled and "set up" by collective acts of mourning and ritual. It is projected and counterinvented by a collective response to the sense of relativization (ambiguity and confusion between the realms of living and dead, between human action and the innate) brought on by the occurrence of death. Since death, as a part of the innate, is compelled by human action, people feel compromised in their inability to prevent it, and so resort to collective ("ritual") action.

"Doing" the innate and collective, drawing the all-important distinction that is the essence of the conventional, is a desperate and fearful act in these societies, whether one "represents" a ghost or spirit-being to others or tells God, with palms pressed together, that He is great and one is unworthy. It invokes the awesome powers of universal creativity in the context of man's ordinary life, and poses the problem of containing and controlling them: the problem of the soul in peril.

Learning humanity

Just as our notions of Culture and collective enterprise are a poor guide to the understanding of peoples who regard their conventions as innate, so the concepts of personality and the individual self, the Freudian id, ego, and superego, are less than helpful in coming to terms with their invention of self. We are dealing here with a world of action and motivation that is in all respects a complete inversion of our own. The definitive sense of "self" precipitated in tribal, peasant, and ethnic "differentiating" traditions is that of an innate spark of conventional discernment, of moral "rightness" or humanity, called the "soul." It is experienced as a seemingly "internal," malleable, and highly vulnerable manifestation of the conventional order implicit in all things: a personal anthropomorphic essence (the form given to man when he was made "in God's image"). To put it simply, the soul sums up the ways in which its possessor is similar to others, over and above the ways in which he differs from them. It comes into being as an inadvertent result of the actor's efforts to differentiate himself, as a felt, motivating "resistance" to those efforts, a thing that guides and inspires his deliberate individuation.

Like the social and existential states and relationships that these people "recognize" and "respond to" in their differentiating acts of joking, avoidance, "doing" maleness or femaleness, or naming, the soul is perceived as a thing existing prior to these acts—*though it is actually invented in the course of doing them.* The soul is precipitated in the course of recognizing and responding to things, *and is experienced as that which recognizes and responds.* It knows itself. The Daribi say that the soul (the seat of man's awareness and speech, and also of his vital functions, which resides in the heart and works through the lungs and liver) grows in an infant and can be recognized in a child when it begins to speak and show explicit discernment. It is then, of course, that the child is able to precipitate its similarity to others, its capability of cultural interpretation, in a recognizable and meaningful way.

The soul is convention precipitated as the self. As such it is passive, a kind of elemental and a priori "conscience," and its motivation takes the form of choosing among alternative solutions or courses of action, rather than initiating action. It is a thing of knowledge rather than power. Just as the Western self, the "id," relies on the artificial constraints and knowledge of Culture to give it direction and orientation (i.e., to precipitate it), so the soul relies on impinging "powers" and influences (including types of magic, spiritual "guidance") to give it impetus and energy (and thus also precipitate it). It motivates by *choosing* its form of activation. One who lives as a soul does so in a world of alternative "ways," "roads to enlightenment"—numerous differentiating controls as means to the fulfillment (and creation) of the self. It is a world of cult, not of alternative moralities so much as alternative roads or means to morality; its important events are choices and realizations rather than deeds.

But among the courses of activation from which the soul must choose are those that involve the deliberate articulation of the conventional, as a countermeasure to the threat of relativization. The soul ultimately *is* the distinction between the innate and the artificial— for this is the very core of its discernment—and so it "inverts" the mode of objectificaton in order to defend this essence and the moral order it represents. When the image of the collective self is used in this way, as a collectivizing control, it is known as "honor," "courtesy," "humanity." Australian aborigines speak of the "track" or way of man, and Daribi myth deals with the "true man" (*bidi mu*) or "straight fellow" (*saregwa*). It is conscious convention, the "straight and narrow" path of moral restoration and emulation, the role of the social and religious leader or lawgiver, of the chief, priest, saint, shaman, seer, or curer. It is also the "way" of courtesy and correct ritual action taken by the ordinary person when confounded and confronted by the threat of ambiguity.

As a collectivizing role, this "honor" or "humanity" precipitates a differentiating motivation, a counterinvention of dynamic, inventive force, which may be identified with an impulsive aspect of the personal constitution (a "body soul," desires "of the flesh" or "of the world") or with some spiritual agency. "Honor" or "humanity" is an acting moral self, a demonstration of "soul," responding to and recognizing (and, of course, creating) its motivating antithesis. As an experience, this motivating "resistance"—the ways in which one's actions fail to conform to the image of the control—takes the form of *shame*. Shame is a manifestation of inappropriate moral awareness, a private or public embarrassment of one's innate humanity, as demonstrated in collectivizing action.

The social relationships of tribal, peasant, and religious peoples, insofar as they are deliberately performed or brought into awareness, are subject to a shaming motivation. Sexuality and sexual intercourse, *when placed in the context of affinal or other social relationships,* are inherently shaming for the Daribi and many another people of this sort; they are *discovered* (whether legitimate or not) and the participants shamed, or they are invoked (when profanity is used) with the intent to shame. The fear of shame, and the omnipresence of potentially shaming situations, is a kind of permanent inducement to moral action in such a society. It puts people "on their moral mettle," so to speak, and triggers the inversion to a defensive, moral stance.

Like guilt among middle-class Americans, shame is a universal device and ploy of interpersonal relations in these societies. People shame each other into responding, doing, giving, and receiving. The elicitation of male roles through female ones (and vice versa), the initiation of a collective task or undertaking, the presentation and acceptance or rejection of wealth in "reciprocity" are all acts of explicit or implicit shaming, or moral challenge and response. "Are you a real man (woman); are you a genuine human being? Then respond morally to this moral situation!" The personal styles of suave composure and buffoonery that I recognized very early in my work among the Daribi (and that Bateson characterized as "rational" and "emotional" among Iatmul debaters) are actually ingrained strategies of shaming. The first, a "courtesy" role, puts others on their mettle and elicits an emulative response; the second teases others with an affected and infectuous shamefulness that threatens to become their own unless they respond morally.

Perhaps the best example of shaming strategies is the roles often taken by Daribi in angry single combat. When approached by an antagonist who is "beside himself" with rage, and usually swinging a length of cane, a person will frequently adopt the role of "righteous victim." As the protagonist lays into him, lashing, screaming, and sometimes kicking, the righteous victim retains his composure, stands his ground without striking back, and "encourages" his opponent, saying "go ahead, hit me again (we can all see what kind of person you are)." This of course makes the protagonist even more furious (and thus morally defenseless); he redoubles his efforts (and hence his shame), trying harder and harder to land the blow that will convince everyone of the seriousness of his anger. Should he succeed, a wise "victim" will make himself even more "righteous" by collapsing and feigning death or serious injury, attempting to show everyone that the protagonist's anger was, in reality, all too serious.

The trick of learning humanity, of being able to "do" the soul as courtesy, honor, piety, is the trick of learning to take it—to take oneself—very, very seriously. This means learning, under the appropriate circumstances, not to take shame seriously at all, to be able to *use* shame (by doing the shameful or eliciting it in others) for moral ends. It means learning to sin, for without sin there is no salvation. This explains why and how people who are schooled to value morality so highly can play the buffoon and perform other acts of seemingly outrageous immodesty, how the Enga and Huli of New Guinea, who live in an awesome dread of female pollution, can reproduce themselves at all. Strange as it may seem to middle-class fugitives from the guilt of overt malperformance and disciples of "fair play," it is the knack of compelling a moral and righteous "humanity," an "honor" or "piety," by any means, fair or foul. (It may be more familiar to politicians and others who condone corruption and all sorts of abuses for the sake "of the greater good" or "of national security.") This is the art of "playing with shame" so that the moral can be real and serious, an art that has its informal and conspiratorial schools in every differentiating tradition.

Learning to dare, to take the moral constraints on invention *just casually enough* to permit the kind of free-wheeling improvisatory action that allows a firm but flexible creation of convention, presents the same necessity in these traditions as the learning of personality does in our own. The moral and conventional must be teased, threatened, and cajoled, it must be invented, for this is the only way it can persist at all. But if the freedom of invention is carried to the extreme of not taking convention seriously, of *using* convention for its own ends, then the threat of relativization, of "counterfeiting" convention, arises. We have seen that in traditions like our own, where morality is a matter of deliberate, explicit action, this "counterfeiting" takes the form of neurosis, the construction of private "conventions" that will allow (and demand) the neurotic to fulfill a desired image of self. Its counterpart in traditions where thought and action is a matter of deliberate and explicit differentiation, where morality is innate and implicit, is *hysteria*. The hysteric "does" or dares beyond the tolerable limits of ordinary action, artificially fabricating "innate" powers that will allow (and ultimately command) him to live in a certain social "state." The sense of self as "soul" becomes ambiguous here—a plaything of the individual powers that the victim strives to invoke or control. He falls into a state of "sickness," "possession," trance, or "soulloss," which may also be interpreted as a kind of communion or contact with spirits, with God or the devil, or simply as a succumbing to malign and lurking "influences."

Learning humanity is thus a continuous struggle with hysteria, intensified at certain "critical" or transitional stages, though of course it is seldom conceived as such. It places the individual in a "double bind" of simultaneously having to respect sin, or shame, or pollution for its obvious moral implications and having to do certain sinful, or shameful, or polluting things. Like the learning of personality, learning humanity obliges a person to become ambiguous, to undergo hysteria at certain stages of development so that he may work his way out of it. But because the modality of thought and action in these traditions is the inverse of our own, this development is not treated or conceptualized as a cyclical "growing up" or "growing into" one's role. It is a thing of *crisis* (of "life crisis"), and this critical quality has to do with the nature of the "soul."

It has to do specifically with the soul's vulnerability. For the soul is at once the culture's great mystery, the thing it enhances, searches, nourishes, and compels, and also the very convention that anchors the actor to his world of dialectical invention. It is not only self, but also morality, not only "person," but also a personal relation to the world. Whereas error and excess are expectable tendencies of an individual self, to be "corrected" by discipline and education, the soul, as a comparatively "passive" quality of discernment, can only be "lost." And when the soul is lost, the only recourse is to *restore* it, to "find" it, rather in the way that a perspective or insight is "found," and not to constrain or educate it. A soul is not disciplined. As the possessor's "touch" and rapport with others and with society, the thing perceived as "soul" is constantly being transformed in the course of inventive action, in the implicit and explicit "representation" of it by the actor and others. Should an inappropriate convention be realized and internalized in the course of such objectification, an inventive orientation *out of relation* to convention, then the problems of "possession" or "soul-loss" would become very real for the actor.

Hence the serious concern with representation among those who live as "souls" in a world of spiritual power. Techniques of sorcery have as their object the representation of personal essence through the use of bodily leavings, food, images, and other means, so that the soul of the victim can be "taken" or reconstituted in an unfavorable state. Representations of divine or other spiritual powers can likewise be used to conjure or compel their essences; a capacity that surrounds many forms of religious art with all manner of taboos. The puritanical movements that have so often arisen in the face of imminent secularization carry this notion to the point of iconoclasm—the renunciation of explicit depiction (of the divine, and even of its created world) for fear of an invidious or sacreligious representation.

In a differentiating tradition, life, too, is a matter of correct representation in the form of action, response, and composure, of respecting the soul and recognizing and responding to the existential states that it comes into. Daribi say that the soul of a small child is exceedingly vulnerable, easily "taken" by ghosts or dislodged by loud noises. They treat their children carefully at this age and encourage their rational responses, though occasional flareups and attempts at punishment often reduce a toddler to helpless, hysterical rage. Older children are allowed to run free to a degree that would amaze Americans, and often young boys are covertly encouraged to have homosexual relations with youths, or are seduced by grown women in bush houses. They learn invention, and shame, by imitation and "on their own," and are *expected* to do so.

Because childhood is a time of "weak" soul and consequently strong influences, a freewheeling and imitative learning of life as invention that often strains the limits of convention, the inculcation of "humanity" occurs as a crisis marking the transition to adulthood. Whether it takes the form of initiation, the attainment of a vision, or some combination or modification of these, it is an experience of discernment or enlightenment, of being able to control the powers and influences that have heretofore (necessarily) had their way with one. Like the other "ceremonial" and "ritual" acts of differentiating traditions, it is a critical readjustment of the tension between invention and convention, an affirmative restoration of the latter in the face of relativization. "Growing up" or "becoming adult" in this way is a cure or control of hysteria, of one's own deficiencies in the invention of self and world, in the way that our "personality development" (which is individual) is a cure or control of neurosis. "Growing up" may be helped along by confession (the differentiation of self from sin), by moral guidance, or by the special magic of moral myths that "compel" and crystallize the innate morality of the listener, but it is useless and pointless unless the individual has already learned invention, the thing it constrains, in the mild hysteria of childhood.

The dynamic powers against which a defensive and relativized soul contends, and which initiation and other forms of ritual strive to contain, are manifestations of hysteria. Whether conceived in explicitly anthropomorphic terms or not, these "powers" and "forces" or "spirits" are the masks, the forms in which relativization is experienced, apprehended, conjured, and exorcised. Implicit by-products of a defensive collectivization, they appear in the form of an offensive and highly energetic individuation. Because relativization, the loss of "soul" and of a moral balance between invention and convention that comprises soul and morality, poses the central necessity of their inventive existence, the lives of people and communities in these traditions are seen as a continual interaction with such powers.

Perhaps the most familiar ethnographic example of these dynamic powers is the Polynesian notion of *mana,* the power that is generated through ritual and creative acts and that endangers those who are not qualified or involved in them. Examples of similar concepts could be cited in the literature on tribal peoples in virtually every other part of the world. Among the Papuans of Kiwai Island in New Guinea the construction of the large communal house, or *dárimo,* was thought to use up the life-force of two elderly people selected as its "parents." And even upon completion, according to the ethnographer Gunnar Landtman, the house was felt to call out perpetually for the deaths of enemies, even rousing its inhabitants at night. It ". . . is an efficient ally of the tribesmen when away on a fighting expedition, for it helps

them from a distance." [6] In its construction the Kiwai house takes on
a force and a motivation of its own, using up the energies of others
and even crying out for more deaths.

A world in which the self takes the form of a passive discernment,
surrounded and threatened by dynamic powers and influences, virtually cries out for the human mastery of its forces. Personal as well as
communal well-being requires that *someone* bring these forces under
control and effect a moral rather than a catastrophic "representation"
of them. For the Melanesians, there is power in death, in dreams, in
peripheral bush spirits and the arcane realm of spells and cult secrets.
For many North American peoples, the species and phenomena of
the outdoor world *were* powers. Often the familiar plants, birds, in-
sects, and mammals represented only a partial sample of the range of
"powers" believed to be present in the universe. Each of these was a
specific manifestation of a generalized "power," with its own secrets,
habits, traits, songs, and so on, and this power could be tapped by
the human being who attained rapport with it (often initiated by a
vision). There was a potentially unlimited range of possibilities for
the personal enhancement entailed by a devotee's association with his
"power," and the procedures involved in seeking and maintaining rapport furnished a guide (and a control) for this enterprise. Among many
groups, such as the Athapascans of the Southwest or the Sioux and
numerous other "historical" Plains tribes, this kind of power was
essential to the success of the ambitious man—much as "education" is
to his professional Western counterpart.

The individual who would learn to compel and control this power
over the collective, the chief, the priest, ritual specialist, monk, curer,
or shaman, must learn to "do" the collectivizing acts by which it is
precipitated without invoking the nuisance of shame or the paralyzing
dread of possession and victimization by the powers. He must learn
an *inversion* of conventional action, transferring the seriousness that
is usually accorded the conventional and the moral to the demands
of his "power," *while not appearing to do so.* He must carry the tendencies of his hysteria "all the way," to the point of *being* (attaining
complete rapport, or union with) his power, but also strive to maintain the image of humanity. For the problem here is not a matter of
losing effective contact and disappearing into a world of one's own;
it is rather one of losing one's moral motivation.

This is the classic dilemma of the African chief, who must be powerful and also moral, exemplified so poignantly by the figure of Yabo

6. Gunnar Landtman, *The Kiwai Papuans of British New Guinea* (London:
Macmillan, 1927), p. 21.

in *Return to Laughter*.[7] It is also the dilemma of the Siberian and North American shaman, who may be obliged to do away with his own kin as a test of his fidelity to his "power" or spirit familiar. It is the predicament of the priest, monk, or nun, who must renounce kin and "worldly" ties. And it is often a source of great anxiety to the others living in these societies, whose lives and well-being are utterly dependent upon a moral invocation and application of the powers. The Daribi, who regard their shamans, or *sogoyezibidi,* with great honor, say that a ghost will choose someone of good judgment for such a calling, for otherwise the *sogoyezibidi* might "go around making people sick."

The situation of such "doers of the collective," whose very souls are articulated as a relation, a kind of "bridge," between the world of innate powers and that of human life, is no less a "double bind" than the situation of a creative individual in Western society. They must treat the conventional casually, yet not appear to do so. And although the ordinary person, in the learning of sin or shame that must accompany his learning of humanity, does this to some degree, the career of the successful chief, priest, or shaman must carry it through to the extent of a complete inversion He must learn to live a completely inverted order of motivation and experience, doing what others regard as innate, while maintaining his social and moral relations with them. In short he is obliged, like his Western counterpart, to continually trick others in the ways they have learned, all unknowingly, to trick themselves—to live a life of obviation that is the way to enlightenment.

As the ordinary course of development, of "learning humanity" in these societies, involves the creation and overcoming of hysterical symptoms, so the road to power or enlightenment involves succumbing to hysteria completely in order to overcome its limitation. This is a more severe hysteria, that comes upon the novice in mature or post-adolescent years, often in the form of illness, seizures, possession, or a "calling" or vocation. Living it out to completion entails continual sickness, frequent fits—a struggle with one's illness, possessing spirit, or vocation until some control over it is achieved: one "dies" and is "born again," one "cures oneself," one "marries Christ" or attains union with some spiritual being. The "cure" is a struggle to reestablish a balance between invention and convention—in this case by reversing the orthodox one.

The "illness or "possession" is conceived as a victimization of the conventional self, the soul, by the spirit or power. Daribi say that

7. Elenore Smith Bowen, *Return to Laughter* (New York: Doubleday, 1964).

an uncontrolled ghost "eats the liver" of its victim, in order to "make a place for itself." As long as the novice continues to identify with this conventional self, while fabricating the representation of a "spirit" (as uncontrolled invention) that demands him to live in a certain "state," the symptoms will continue, or worsen. He is inventing "against convention," counterfeiting a state of being that conflicts with his soul, his moral motivation. (Daribi women who have lost a husband or a child frequently become novice mediums in this way; they want to keep their souls, and yet also maintain a relationship with the deceased, whose representation as a ghost takes precedence over their own volition.) However, as the novice approaches closer and closer to a situation of "rapport," as he comes to identify with the power and the state that he is "counterfeiting," the hysterical symptoms begin to disappear, the ghost or spirit becomes more "controlled" and less unruly. Finally, when full identification is achieved, the former novice is able to precipitate the motivation of the ghost or spirit *as his own*, and thus to attempt the collectivizing acts through which it is precipitated without fear of victimization. His actions, the morality that he deliberately "builds," become a kind of lightning rod, a conductor of spiritual power.

chapter 5

The invention of society

Cultural "change": Social convention as inventive flow

We have been focusing thus far on the viewpoint of the actor—the inventor—in the universal phenomenon of cultural invention. And even if we keep in mind the provision that the actor in any situation can be a person, part of a person, a group, or some other culturally recognized entity, the actor is always placed in *some* relation to convention. He may "do" convention in the sense of deliberately articulating conventional contexts, or he may *subsume* convention as the implicit context of his action, he may in fact "counterfeit" a conventional world of his own, but the conventional is always a factor. The way in which he conceives of his motivation in relation to his invention (his control), the "illusion" to which he is necessarily subject in the course of action, is dictated by cultural convention. And in analyzing the phenomenon of invention from the viewpoint of the actor, it has been necessary to regard the conventions of his culture—what is understood to be "innate" as opposed to what is seen as the "artificial" realm of human manipulation—as relatively static.

Thus I have obliged the reader to regard the existence of collectivizing and differentiating "traditions" or conventional modes as "givens." But a realization of the profound conceptual and experiential differences between the two forces into prominence the question of how things came to be that way, of how this profound differentiation of mankind came into existence and how and why it changes or maintains itself. This, the problem of cultural "change," or, in its broadest dimensions, that of cultural "evolution," amounts to what I shall call that of the "invention of society."

The problem is not "evolutionary" in the ordinary anthropological or sociobiological sense, for there is nothing necessarily "primitive" about a differentiating "ideology," and nothing necessarily "advanced" about a collectivizing one. Over and above the fact that all people, regardless of social class or allegedly "civilized" status, from time to time undertake both modes of action, the probability that urban man's forebears all lived in differentiating regimes is *not* a sign of their evolutionary priority or "primitiveness." On the contrary, all the more "mature" and long-established civilizations that we know of emphasize differentiating or dialectical modes of thought and action. And this fact makes our own traditional obsession with "evolution"—with invention disguised as "progress"—problematic, and gives a timely urgency to the question of the invention of society.

This is why I have chosen to pitch my discussion of human symbolization in the broadest terms possible. When the contradictory and often unimaginable aspects of "cultural difference" occur in the course of much more sensitive and particular studies of specific conceptual worlds, such as those of Ruth Benedict and Oswald Spengler (to mention only two, very controversial, instances), they are frequently cast into the limbo of the "merely symbolic," or patronized with the platitudes about "seeing" or "classifying" the world differently. Differentiating and collectivizing modes of action, and of course all human thought and action, are invariably contingent upon specific contexts, specific idioms, and specific symbols. The tendency of analyst and reader alike has been to lose oneself in this specificity, to become so charmed by the force of exotic idioms that one's overall perspective is lost to a general sense of relativistic ambiguity, or a certainty of "organic cultures fulfilling their destinies." "Differentiation" and "collectivization" are overriding abstractions. That is why I use them.

The conventions that determine which of these is to be the understood and morally approved style of human action are themselves dependent upon invention for their own continuity. Whether implicitly or explicitly, convention is reinvented again and again in the course of action. Of course, since its continuance is predicated upon invention, it may often be reinvented in ways that depart somewhat from earlier representations. Most of these departures, whether gradual or precipitous, collective or individual, amount to mere alterations of imagery, like the cult ideologies of tribal peoples, or clothing styles in America. But when changes occur that serve to alter the distinction between what is innate and what is artificial, we can speak of a significant conventional change. In individual instances, this amounts to the "counterfeiting" of convention that is a part of the "trial and error" of growing up, or even the neurosis or hysteria of an adult. And it may culminate in a total inversion of cultural convention on the part of a leader or creative person, or that of a schizophrenic or paranoiac.

The more momentous alterations of convention are social ones, however, involving large numbers of people through the very bases of their intercommunication. They are, in fact, inevitable, owing to the exchange of characteristics that must invariably accompany objectification. Languages literally "talk themselves" into other languages, and societies live themselves into new social forms. If we understand these symptoms as consequences of the use of ambiguous and relativized controls, rather than conditions of the individual "mind" or "psyche," then we may characterize the behavior of whole social movements and even of societies in terms of "neurosis," "hysteria," or conventional inversion. For collectively held conventions are no less dependent upon invention than personal conventions, and when people subscribe collectively to a certain distinction between the innate and the artificial, and yet employ relativized controls that obviate the distinction, they precipitate a collective crisis.

This situation typifies modern America, where the realm of human action has become "automatic" and bureaucratized beyond the point of responsible "accountability," whereas that of the innate requires constant human intervention (in terms of conservation, medication, and so forth). Relativization occurs among tribal and religious peoples too, appearing as the "powerlessness" of ritual forms of action in the face of spiritual turmoil, of the gods and spirits getting out of hand. And insofar as all human action is motivated by the need to counteract relativization, this most extreme and universal manifestation of relativization presents the most pressing necessity of all—the need to invert one's mode of action and restore the conventional balance. The longer a complete and effective restoration is delayed or postponed by "halfway" measures (such as advertising and other "interpretive" activities, programs for "conservation" and partial reorganization), the more urgent this necessity becomes.

People literally invent themselves out of their conventional orientations, and the way in which this tendency is counteracted and dealt with is the key to their social and historical self-manipulation, to their invention of society. But before we deal with the far-reaching implications of this invention, it would be helpful to gain some understanding of cultural convention as a kind of movement or inventive flow, a "communicational" basis supported entirely by inventive effort. Let us consider the example of language.

The invention of language

The set of conventions by which certain sounds or groups of sounds are understood to "stand for" certain culturally recognized experiences and things, and by which these sounds are ordered and transformed to articulate meaningful expression—this commonly held body of "agreements" which we call "language"—is always part of the collective aspect of culture. Language in its lexical, grammatical, and rhetorical distinctions is always part of the moral, and belongs to the (relatively) conventionalized contexts of a culture. In traditions where these conventional contexts are felt to represent the "given" nature of being human, language is also considered to be part of this innate humanity. The sound of a word is thought to have some intrinsic relation to the things it conventionally "stands for," so that by uttering a verbal spell one exercises a kind of control over the things referred to in the spell. (Thus the Daribi gardener in our example could believe he was actually taking on characteristics of the bushfowl.) In traditions where the conventionalized contexts define the domain of human action, such as our own, language is felt to be an arbitrary product of historical development, something that people can actually "make up." Thus we often speak of languages as "codes," and consistently underestimate the difficulty of "translating" from one language to another.

Whether they are perceived as "given" and immutable, or assumed and manipulable, the grammars, vocabularies, syntaxes, and rhetorical usages of language serve as a collective basis for communication. They are conventionalized contexts for the expression of meaning; people must come to terms with them, within certain limits of tolerance, if they are to be understood. But although the formal elements and distinctions are necessary to verbal expression, they are not sufficient in themselves. After all, there must be something to talk about. The elements and distinctions of language are not intrinsically meaningful, though they can be used to elicit meaning, or can be elicited by its expression. The conventions of language become meaningful only when they enter into relations of objectification with some observed or imagined context (when they objectify it, or are objectified by it).

When a linguist makes up a sentence like "the boy bit the dog," he is eliciting an imaginary context to illustrate the meaningful "use" of language. If, however, engrossed in the bizarre situation, he should shout, "Look, look, he's *biting* the poor mutt!," he would be objectifying language by the context of its application.

The involvement of language in meaningful expression, which the structuralists and structural linguists call "speech" (*parole*), thus amounts to objectification. The conventions of language must be "metaphorized" through some interrelation with situational phenomena (the context of speech, "the world") if they are to produce meaning. As we have seen, this metaphorization can come about in two ways: language can serve as the objectifier (the control) or as the thing objectified (the context that is controlled). (In the terminology of those who deal with metaphor, language can be either the *vehicle*, the control, or the *tenor*, that which is controlled.) Although both kinds of metaphorization are found in all traditions, we should not be surprised to discover that urban Westerners stress the use of language as a control, whereas tribal, peasant, and lower-class urban peoples control language through expressive formulations (through their use of the world, we might say).

Where, as in our own society, language is felt to be a thing of conscious rules and performance (the "use" of language), the subjects of speech are objectified directly through the elements and distinctions of language. They are given collectively understood associations through the words and articulative forms the speaker uses. We invent an incidental and historical or situational "reality" through the conscious use of language, one that demands "correct usage" from the speaker. If language is arbitrary and capable of correction and change for us, the world of "fact" and "event" is definitely nonarbitrary: our scientific, legal, and historical investigations are (inventive) efforts to find out "what the facts are" and "what really happened." Like the rational methodologies of these disciplines, we require our language to be a precision instrument (albeit one of our own making) for the description and representation of a stubbornly factual world, and our view of language in general often reflects this bias.

Where language is felt to be a "given" reality in itself, something (like morality) that is manifested in a person's actions but not consciously "used" or "corrected," we find a different orientation of communication and expression. Here meaning is produced by the objectification (and invention) of language, as a collectivity, through the subjects being discussed. The problems and occasions of "speech" take precedence over those of "language," which emerges as a *result* of expression. People elicit the subjects of speech metaphorically in such a way that the general conventions of language are satisfied; language is not "used" so much as the subjects of discussion are. These nonconventionalized controls are employed as objectifiers, giving their disparate characteristics to the commonly accepted distinctions and elements of language in such a way as to metaphorize them and turn them into meaning.

This "inverse" orientation to verbal expression gives ordinary speech the colorful and consciously metaphoric character that we associate with the "style" of American Indians, cockney slang, and the imagery of American blacks. Speech becomes a matter of conscious differentiation rather than literal performance. This usage corresponds to a view of the world as phenomenally inchoate and subject to the constructions that people put upon it. It has its regularities, to be sure, but these are in turn dependent (in the particular forms they assume) upon the ways people choose to articulate them and bring them into relation with the collective. The characteristics of the world are "hidden" and must be revealed by metaphorizing them in such a way that they will turn into the commonly understandable and communicable conventions of language. The most frequently used metaphorizations will give the world a semblance of conventional form and structure, but this is always open to revision as newer constructions come into prominence or take the place of older ones. It is a "world as hypothesis" that need never suffer the stringencies of final "proof" or legitimation, an *unscientific* world. This is why tribal peoples can recognize and give credence to mutually contradictory mythic accounts of the world's origin and structure with perfect equanimity.

Like the other components of our collective Culture, language is a means of rationalizing the world, of inventing it as a causal continuum of fact and event. Our language is a conventionalized control placed in a determinate relation to other such controls. For tribal, peasant, and other nonrationalistic traditions, language takes its place among the collective contexts that are controlled and invented, objectified through the alternative controls of the experiential world. In the first case language gives the characteristics of conventional order to the world, transforming it into meaning and understandable relations; in the second case language takes individual and differentiating characteristics from the world, and is thus transformed into meaning. But in both cases the conventional orders and distinctions that constitute language are involved in an *exchange of characteristics* with the set of alternative controls that make up the subjects of speech (the "world"), for the long-term effects of control are those of turning nonconventionalized contexts into conventionalized ones, and vice versa. Under the impress of countless speech events and constructions the individual metaphors and other analogous expressions of ordinary speech slowly turn into the conventions of language, which become particularized and lose their conventional status.

Thus the absolutely conventional (or "correct") nature of lexical and grammatical distinctions as well as the absolutely nondetermined and voluntary nature of expressive constructions (like metaphors, figures of speech, and the sentences that contain them) is always something of an illusion. The conventions of language are always to some extent relative, for as an element in the ongoing invention of the world, language itself is always in the process of being invented. There are generally more alternative "correct" ways of making linguistic distinctions, and fewer meaningful though different ways of describing a situation or phenomenon, than any speaker of a language is aware of. This is because any given speaker or community of speakers must maintain an image and a practice of what is conventional and what is nonconventionalized in the way of language usage, just as they must with regard to the other contexts of culture.

Instead of a bounded set of conventions (syntactic, grammatical, and lexical) that can be rearranged in various combinations to describe the world and its situations, every language constitutes a spectrum of more or less conventionalized sound forms, ranging from purely systematic distinctions (like those of syntax and grammar) to evocative analogic constructions that "describe" (and invent) the world of speech. At one extreme is the set of distinctions and precedents that order and arrange the fact of verbal articulation itself through their systematic contrasts, though the order they manifest is that of convention alone and has no expressive "content." At the other extreme are expressive constructs that use one control or another in the objectifying activity of "speech." These constructs have an expressive content that is distinct from the conventional forms through which they are ordered. This content, and indeed the control that is used in its objectification, may in fact be very much conventionalized or even commonplace from the standpoint of the speaker's culture, but as long as it remains distinct as the subject of speech it will not enter the conventional order of language. When, however, we begin to use such a construct as a "figure of speech" in contexts outside those of its original expression, when we make its imagery a part of our imagery of saying things in general, it becomes one conventionally recognized "way of saying something."

The use of a figurative construct to facilitate the formation of other figurative constructs, however seldom or sporadic, amounts to the linguistic conventionalization of what was formerly a nonconventionalized control. What was previously a part of the content of speech has entered the range of relatively conventionalized forms that grade between expressive constructs and the systemic orders of syntax and grammar. It is difficult to determine whether clichés like "from my point of view" or "for the time being" ought to belong to "language" or not. They are conventionalized to the point where most speakers know what they mean, or even expect them, yet they retain an alternative character because other arrangements of words may be freely substituted for them without altering the "correctness" or linguistic acceptability. Their analogic relationship to the original contexts within the realm of speech is also apparent—for we draw upon this "imagery" in using them: "point of view" conjures up an image of the relative changes in appearance of an object when seen from different angles. Yet this imagery is often so dulled by constant use (conventionalization) that it comes to be "taken for granted" and lost. People often classify such "figures of speech" as part of rhetoric, or "language use," but they are good examples of the relativity of conventional controls.

Words, likewise, are formed by the conventionalization of analogic constructs, and the relative conventionalization of a word can be measured by the degree to which its metaphoric basis remains obvious. "Flying saucer" is still "new" in this regard, and retains something of its original metaphoric significance, but "airplane," "ice cream," and "housewife" represent more firmly entrenched conventionalizations, and we do not ordinarily consider their analogic origins unless something calls our attention to them. Finally the analogic basis of "culture" is only apparent in the similarity of this word to the forms of "cultivate," while words like "house" and "wife" have long passed beyond the pale of any sort of analogic recognition. Often, acronyms (abbreviations or initials like "Nazi," "FBI," "UFO," or "VD") or combinations of words taken from other languages (like "television," "automobile," or "telekinesics") are used to facilitate the conventionalization of new constructs by blurring their analogic bases or making them comparatively inaccessible. Yet the conventionalization of words, like that of other kinds of constructs, is understandable as part of a gradual process of conventionalizing the controls used alternatively (whatever their conventional status in the culture at large) in creating the "content" of speech. It is as difficult to determine the boundaries of a language's vocabulary as it is to delimit its other formal elements.

Conventionalization continues to work upon the semianalogical constructs that form the vague and fluid "boundary" of language, but in a selective way, so that the more commonly used ones eventually lose their figurative nature altogether and become part of the systemic order of syntax, grammar, or lexicon. Our use of the auxiliaries "have" and "will" to form the past and future tenses of verbs exemplifies this. These verbs have all but lost their respective senses of "possessing" or "willing" (volition) in such grammatical contexts, though it is still possible to imagine how they came to be selected for these uses (since "possessing" implies past action, and "volition" implies future action). Other systemic aspects of language, such as the verbal inflections -ed and -ing, or the elements of English word order, do not even permit this degree of analogic reconstruction, except perhaps by experts. But conventionalization continues to operate even upon these most highly abstracted and systematized elements of language, regularizing aberrant forms and drawing them more consistently into a pattern. Comprehensive and well-chosen examples of this process in English and other languages can be found in Edward Sapir's excellent study *Language*.[1]

Concurrent with the process of linguistic conventionalization in all degrees of relative conventionality, a counterprocess of differentiating or particularizing the conventions of language is always at work. Whether the elements of language are actively used as a control or serve as a context for other controls, encounters with the particular contexts of speech have the effect of objectifying them and giving them highly specific characteristics. When some particular word, phrase, or grammatical element occurs frequently in one context to the exclusion of others, it takes on the peculiar associations of that context— eventually to the extent of losing its conventional status. We might say that general linguistic elements become "specialized" in this way —they are "selected," consciously or unconsciously, for use in certain contexts so that eventually most of their meaningful associations come from those contexts.

Sometimes this selection represents a general tendency on the part of the speakers of a language, so the words or grammatical or rhetorical forms change in their overall linguistic significance. In other instances the selection represents the preferences and usages of some particular social, educational, or occupational context, or some social class or regional group, resulting in the differentiation of language itself into particular "styles" and dialects. In either instance the process operates to particularize and differentiate the collective properties of language through the diverse contents and situations of speech to "deconventionalize" them in one way or another.

Individual words, phrases, and grammatical usages are often par-

---

1. Edward Sapir, *Language: An Introduction to the Study of Speech* (New York: Harcourt Brace Jovanovich, 1921).

ticularized to the degree that their conventional applicability is gradually restricted. There is evidence that our word "deer" once referred to animals in general, like its German cognate "Tier"—Shakespeare speaks of "mice and other small deer." Subsequently the word has been employed so exclusively in reference to a few particular species that "deer" has much more restricted associations for us now. Similarly the word "notorious" was once a fairly "neutral" synonym for "famous" or "publicly known," but has gradually taken on ominous connotations through a tendency to apply it exclusively in the cases of evil-doers. Likewise figures of speech often come to have a very specific contextual significance: ships (but not aircraft or automobiles) can "put out," "stand out," or "stand to," while automobiles can "run down" but ships cannot.

The contexts in which language is applied may be socially or regionally differentiated as well as topically distinct, and this kind of differentiation also has its effects on the objectification of linguistic elements. The vocabulary and rhetoric of the traditional British "upper classes" was long subject to an objectification from French and Latin usages, since contact with these languages was a significant feature in the context of aristocratic and professional life. Thus "upper-class" English became differentiated as a social dialect distinct from the styles of tradesmen, laborers, or countrymen from various parts of the island. The latter, however, spoke regional dialects, forms of English that had become objectified through the contextual presence of Celtic, Nordic, or other Germanic idioms. And even where such "influences" are not a factor, the contextual distinctness of social, occupational, and regional speech communities exercises a differentiating effect upon the conventions of language. American professionals speak a fairly standardized "class" dialect, heavily influenced by the "academese" of their education and the standardized idioms of journalism. Beyond this, and especially among nonprofessionals, "American English" undergoes a continual differentiation into regional, occupational, and colloquial jargons and dialects.

Both the linguistic conventionalization of ordinary speech constructs, by which a collective language is formed, and the differentiation of conventional linguistic usages, by which it is fragmented and particularized (and dialects, individual "languages," are formed), contribute to an ongoing relativity of linguistic convention. Because they are necessary consequences of objectification, and because speech is necessarily a process of objectifying, conventional relativity is a permanent attribute of all living languages. A language can never become static or definitely bounded; it is always drawing in figurative constructs from speech and gradually assimilating them to its conventional format, and always losing the conventional and communicable viability of elements as they undergo gradual particularization. The relativity of linguistic convention is a consequence of ongoing and necessary change.

But this relativity is almost never apparent to those who live with a language. For them the objectification of language and of its subjects carries the same implications and consequences as other kinds of objectification—that is, it bears directly upon their "being" and "doing" and upon the motivations involved in these. If we choose to abstract and simplify linguistic conventionalization and particularization to the point of calling them "processes," then we must keep in mind that such "processes" are completely and invariably embodied in human motivation and invention, for language can no more exist outside of the emotional and creative situations of human life than culture can. Under varying circumstances language can take the form of a collectivizing control, motivated by the invention of "speech," or it can serve as a conventional motivation precipitated by the imagery of speech.

Where language is ordinarily employed as a collectivizing control, the objectification of its formal contexts is experienced as the expectable result of "natural" tendencies (like those of the "natural" self). Middle-class Americans regard as inevitable the effects of their historical and factual world upon language (word and phrase changes through change in technology, "influence," or environment; jargon and dialect formation as the result of specialization or isolation). By the same token they are motivated to counteract these "natural" changes by consciously collectivizing: compiling and using dictionaries and grammatical texts, teaching and learning their language, contriving acronyms and other artificially "conventionalized" forms, and creating "standardized" dialects, artificial languages, codes, and information-processing systems in the interest of "communication."

When one's ordinary linguistic resources fail, either because one is still "learning" the language and cannot do justice to a particular speech situation, or because available forms are conventionalized to the point of being "trite," one is forced to invert the controls and "invent language" by deliberately articulating (metaphoric) "speech" constructions. This inversion, a linguistic equivalent of the "conscious invention" that we call "personality," is as important in learning to speak as it is in learning to be a self. It is especially characteristic of the speech of small children (which we might want to call "linguistic play"), and amounts to the formally invisible aspect of speaking that

Noam Chomsky has characterized as "performance" in contrast to the "competence" of deliberate grammatical and syntactic construction. "Performance" is simply the ability to articulate the "world," the imagery of differentiating speech constructs; it is the "poetry" that romanticists imagined as the original form of language. It is invented as an "innate" and compelling mystery (like "personality" or "evolution") by the linguists' single-minded concentration on the formal and conventional aspects of speech (their "linguage," as I call it, in its many dialects: transformational and rewrite "rules," clever notational systems, and so on).

Among peoples whose languages ordinarily take the role of that which is objectified and counterinvented through the diverse individual controls of the world, conventionalization (the objectification of those controls) is understood to be "given" and inevitable, regardless of man's action. "In the beginning was the Word, and the Word was with God, and the Word was God": like the other aspects of man's collectivity, language is regarded as an innate property of man's existence by peasant, tribal, and religious peoples. Its "invention" through the conventionalization of the world comes about "naturally" through the ordinary acts of living in a society. "Eat our pandanus fruit, smoke our tobacco," the Daribi people told me, "and you will know our language." But this same "automatic" transformation of the world into conventional homogeneity motivates the individual speaker to distinguish his own identity and effective action from those of others. Thus he will consciously differentiate his speech, emphasizing the expressive power and peculiarity of what he has to say by building its figurativeness through the use of all sorts of bizarre and exotic controls. The result may be "magic" or poetry, or simply that amazing indirection of discourse that alternately enchants and mystifies those Westerners who presume to construe it as deliberate "communication."

When this mode of speaking fails to communicate in some significant sense, when it ceases to be intelligible, the speaker is obliged to invert his objectification of language and turn to a conscious linguistic "competence." He makes explicit linguistic distinctions, defining words by pointing to objects and "denoting" them, or clarifying grammatical or syntactic usages. Like "performance" in our own society, this "competence" is a necessary part of learning to speak for members of a differentiating tradition, and it is thus particularly characteristic of children (though "denoting" is often an important feature of initiation rites). Adult Daribi would frequently chuckle at the sight of a toddler tirelessly and methodically listing food plants for me, or pointing to objects and telling me their names. But the same adults would find it necessary, on other occasions, to help the outsider by explaining verbal contractions, or pointing out significant actions and objects and telling me their local names.

Thus "performance" and "competence," the use of differentiating and collectivizing controls respectively, as well as the inversions involved in switching from one mode to the other, are necessary for the learning of speech in any culture. They may, of course, be "weighted" differently in different traditions, depending on the respective conventions as to what is innate and what is artificial. Learning to speak in a language means learning to maintain the boundary between the forms of speech and its contents through ongoing acts of articulation; it is a continual struggle against the relativization of language on one hand, and that of speech constructs on the other. The acts of objectification, through which this relativity is masked and the boundary between linguistic form and content is maintained, can only lead to further relativization. Speech, in other words, creates the ongoing change of language through the very means by which an illusion of stability is maintained, and linguistic form lives in an inventive flux as much as the imagery of speech constructs does.

This situation bears significant implications for the invention of society generally, and since this discussion of language is intended largely as an illustration of cultural convention as inventive "flow," we will follow these implications back to our main theme. But before we leave the subject of language it is important to remind ourselves that we used language and speech merely as *examples* of the broader phenomena of objectification and control. When I speak of conventionalization or differentiation of linguistic forms, I mean that these forms become conventional or particularized *with regard to the issue of speaking and verbal articulation.* Though they share thereby in the social, political, and emotional significances that language has for us, these transformations are not *necessarily* equivalent to the ones that speech represents. The imagery of language, or saying things in general, has a different function or intent than the imagery of what is said, however much they may overlap. To borrow a felicitous example from Christian Morgenstern, one cannot really conjugate a werewolf into "willwolf," "wouldwolf," "shouldwolf," and so forth.

Language is an aspect of culture that can be used to represent virtually the whole of cultural life, though in the process its conventional forms must be kept distinct. Myth, art, mathematics, iconography, and even the specialized "linguage" of linguists are analogous aspects, living in the tension and interaction between conventional form and representational extension. So was music for Richard Strauss, who boasted that he was capable of letting the listener know whether the subject of one of his tone poems was using a fork or a spoon.

The invention of society

There are two possible ways in which the relationship between the conventions of culture and the dialectic of invention can be maintained. Either the dialectic can be used consciously to mediate the conventional forms, or the articulation of conventionalized contexts into a conscious unity can be used to mediate the dialectic. Each of these modes corresponds to a particular kind of cultural continuity, to a particular conception of self, society, and world, and to a particular set of problems that confront (and motivate) the inventors. Dialectical thought and action addresses itself consciously to the mechanics of *differentiation* against a background of similarity; collectivizing or rationalist approaches emphasize integration and the element of similarity against a background of differences. Since the dialectic embodies the means of cultural change and continuity, cultures that use the dialectic to mediate their conventional forms will maintain an inherent stability of a kind that is inaccessible to those that mediate the dialectic through conventional forms.

What do I mean by "mediate," and how does this matter relate to stability and continuity? Mediation refers to the use of one thing, or one kind of thing, as a means to doing something else—the use of one context to control another is an example of mediation. But here I am talking about abstract ways of managing the interaction of controls—about the use of one *kind* of control (conventionalized or nonconventionalized, as the case may be) as a basis of orientation for self-invention of a people or tradition as a whole. The problem of the invention of society involves the maintenance or change of this orientation. Cultures that mediate the conventional dialectically make differentiation (including the qualities of paradox, contradiction, and reciprocal interaction) the basis of their thought and action. They play out the dialectical and motivational contradictions consciously in their management of roles, rituals, and situations, and thus continually reconstitute the conventional. Cultures that mediate the dialectic through the conventional, on the other hand, pattern their thought and action on a model of consistent, rational, and systematic articulation, stressing the avoidance of paradox and contradiction. Drawing upon a familiar Freudian idiom, we might say that they "repress" the dialectic, though in so doing they come to embody it in their own histories—they are "used" by it.

Modern academics might prefer to see this contrast as one of different "logics": a dialectic and temporal (i.e., stressing the changing value of propositions in time) logic versus a linear and nontemporal logic.[2] Yet since many of us have been taught to regard logic as some-how antithetical to emotion and motivation, the term "logic" could prove as dangerous and misleading as Levy-Bruhl's characterization of dialectical thought as "prelogical" or "magical." The effect of such hyperbole (as well as the even less palatable idioms of "primitiveness" and "stone-age man") is to make the issue of *thinking* a paramount feature of our approach to culture. Since thought is inseparable from action and motivation, we are not so much dealing with different "logics" or rationalities as with total modes of being, of inventing self and society. A consciously dialectical mode of invention is characteristic of some of the most sophisticated traditions we know of, and linear, rationalist approaches have also been widespread in great civilizations.

The dialectical nature of thought and action in tribal societies has long been an experience of ethnographers, whatever they chose to make of it theoretically. Whether apprehended as uncanny wisdom (a Daribi man once told me: "A man is small; when you speak his name, he is big") or canny observation (as in the case of that "ecological" Eskimo saying that "the wolf keeps the reindeer strong, and the reindeer keeps the wolf strong"), the comments of his subjects often pinpoint the very dependencies the anthropologist is trying to capture. Writers like Lévi-Strauss have amassed volumes of examples of the dialectical nature of ceremonial in these societies. Perhaps the best overview of the phenomenon can be found in Bateson's remarks on "duality" among the Iatmul of New Guinea:

> . . . We must see the development of alternating systems in Iatmul culture and their absence in our own culture as a function of the fact that among the Iatmul *both* complementary and symmetrical patterns are thought of in dual terms, while in Europe though we regard complementary patterns either as dual or as arranged in hierarchies, we do not think of patterns of rivalry and competition as necessarily dual. Rivalry and competition in our communities are thought of as occurring between any number of persons with no presumption that the resulting system will be patterned upon any sort of bilateral symmetry. Only if both types of relationship are habitually thought of in dual terms is it likely that alternating hierarchies of the Iatmul type will be developed.[3]

2. Those interested in pursuing this distinction as a matter of logic would do well to consult *Laws of Form* by G. Spencer Brown (London: Allen and Unwin, 1969), a brilliant discussion similar to one in an unpublished manuscript by J. David Cole, "An Introduction to Psycho-Serial Systems and Systematics" (1968). Cole comments that "it is not necessary for acts to have ideas behind them; they take their place in any chain of psycho-serial events as parts of rational processes. When we seek the idea behind an action we merely seek to elaborate its meaning" (p. 1).

3. Gregory Bateson, *Naven*, 2nd ed. (Stanford: Stanford University Press, 1958), p. 273.

Like many (but by no means all) tribal peoples, the Iatmul have simplified the ritual (the "inverse" or "antimotivational") aspect of their culture by conceptualizing it in dualistic terms. Accordingly, they furnish a fine example of the dialectical self-invention of tribal society, for they allow the ethnographer to objectify dialectical process in terms of "duality." The collectivizing acts in which the Iatmul create the "givens" of life and recharge the symbols of their ordinary differentiating existence take the form of oppositional and competitive relations between two moieties, or "halves," of the society. They include the *naven* ceremonial, celebrating an individual's self-assertion or achievement of some cultural status (especially a child's "first" acts: first use of an implement, first kill, first act of exchange), the initiation of youths, marriage exchanges, and the ceremonial debates in which the origins and ancestry of the social and phenomenal world are established. All of these have to do with the ritual creation of things: of people (in *naven* ceremonies and initiation); of families (in marriage); and of the social and phenomenal realities of the world (in the ceremonial debates). All are conceptualized and carried out in terms of the dialectical interaction of the two moieties, which both depend on each other and oppose or contradict one another.

Even when they are not conceived in such explicitly dualistic forms, the ritual and "creative" aspects of tribal cultures betray a dialectical conceptualization. The Daribi have no moieties—individual units intermarry with one another at will, yet every marriage involves the opposed roles of "wife-giver" and "wife-taker"—and those that produce offspring lead to relations between the "mother's people" and "father's people" that resemble those of the Iatmul *naven*. When a Daribi community undertakes to reestablish rapport with ghosts that threaten its well-being, it will subdivide into two opposed ritual sections—the *"habu* men" (who take the part of the ghosts) versus the "house men" in the *habu* ceremonial, and the "holders of the *gerua"* versus impersonators of the ghosts in the ceremony of the painted *gerua* board that accompanies a pig-feast. Though they lack the broad, overarching scheme of universally opposed moieties, Daribi maintain the dialectical nature of creative activity through many specific social and ceremonial applications.

Bateson's observations also suggest that the ordinary ("complementary" or differentiating) activities of tribal peoples are understood by them in dialectical terms. Male-female relationships (and for that matter the other forms of individuation and separation) can be seen as acts of conscious differentiation against a background of common similarity (the "soul" and the other collectivities of culture), and thus as a dialectic between the particular and the general, between man and woman, and so on. There are innumerable examples in the anthropological literature to support this suggestion. In *Naven* Bateson discusses at great length the generative opposition ("complementary schismogenesis") beween the personal "style" or ethos of Iatmul men and that of the women, implying that for the Iatmul living as a man or woman involves participation in an essentially dialectical inter- action. The *Jamaa* movement of Katanga, in Africa, which developed out of the confrontation of native conceptual forms with Western attempts at industrialization, states this "domestic" dialectic in epigram- matic form: "The husband shall be born of his wife; the wife shall be born of her husband." [4]

Taken as a whole, then, the self-invention of tribal societies is lived (i.e., *motivated* within the participants) and conceptualized as a creative alternation between two basic sets of relations, each of which is con- ceived in dialectical terms. As Bateson's remarks indicate, the dialec- tical or "dual" nature of each set of relations reflects and reinforces that of the other; the "dualistic" character of Iatmul actions and institutions corresponds to the fact that the Iatmul think and act—and therefore invent themselves and their society—dialectically. They mediate the conventions of their culture through the dialectic, rather than vice versa. The set of relations that encompasses ordinary (dif- ferentiating) activity, identified with the motivations of the self, and the set of relations that corresponds to "ritual" (collectivizing) activity, motivated by the "powers," the anthropomorphic beings and forces that create man's life, and mode of being, stand in a mutually con- tradictory and creative relationship to one another. Thus, in this inherently dialectical conception of man and the world, the totality of things is also understood dialectically; the differentiating oppositions of everyday life (male versus female) both create those of ritual and ceremonial activities (i.e., the "religious" oppositions between man and the "powers" of the world) and are created by them. Each is both inimical and necessary to the other.

The differentiating acts and roles of everyday existence create col- lectivity and community; the collectivizing acts of ritual and cere- monial create the identities, roles, and other differentiating aspects of ordinary existence. Because the alternation between these two modes is itself conceived dialectically, each set of relations can be understood as "working against" the other. The "resistance" to differentiating acts

4. Johannes Fabian, *Jamaa: A Charismatic Movement in Katanga* (Evanston, Ill.: Northwestern University Press, 1971), p. 149. *Jamaa* means "family," and the doc- trine of the movement consciously uses the dialectical concept of "mutual genera- tion" (*ku-zala*, cf. pp. 132, 149) implicit in the husband–wife relationship to char- acterize its unity.

brought about by the collectivizing of the controls motivates the actors to greater efforts at differentiation; the differentiation of collectivizing controls likewise motivates the actors to further attempts at collectivizing. Thus each mode of activity retains the capacity to contradict and negate the other, and each is carried on in such a way that it excludes the other. Ritual and ceremonial elements (masks, costumes, implements, and formulae) are felt to be "dangerous" to domestic relations and circumstances, and are kept apart from them. Ceremonial activities are often carried out in secluded surroundings, free from the "profanation" of ordinary domestic life. Separation of this kind occurs in a bewildering variety of ethnographic forms (such as "men's houses," taboos, withdrawal and ceremonial isolation), but its basic tendency is that of the dialectic itself—to maintain a particular conception and orientation of self in relation to the world of "powers."

Because the two modes are conceived as antithetical, the negation or compromising of one leads automatically to the other. When actions proper to one kind of kin role are included in the performance of another, as in the act of incest, the effect is both to compromise the mode of ordinary differentiation and to "dehumanize" the actor, causing him to invent a nonanthropomorphic self.[5] In parts of New Guinea and Australia the most stringent kin role restrictions involve a man and his wife's mother, and it is significant in the light of this that among the Aranda of Central Australia (where this holds true), some sacred ceremonials include acts of sexual connection between relatives in these categories. The intention, in fact, is precisely that of negating the ordinary mode of activity, so that man's socialized state can be revoked, and the primal "creative" order of things (*alcheringa*) reinstated. In the Daribi *habu* ceremonial, which must be carried on exclusively by the men if it is to succeed, the women appear in men's attire, singing verses in which they beg to be allowed to participate and also taunt the participants. By threatening to "complementarize" a ritual activity along "profane" lines, they put the men "on their mettle" and serve to motivate their performance of the ceremony. Finally, at its conclusion, the women appear again in transvestite garb and carry a pole in noisy procession down the central corridor of the house in which the ceremonial terminates, an act of overt opposition to the men that negates the ceremonial opposition (that of "house men" versus "*habu* men") by reinstating the more ordinary one of male-female complementarity.

Tribal people create self and society episodically, through an al-

---

5. See R. Wagner, "Incest and Identity: A Critique and Theory on the Subject of Exogamy and Incest Prohibition," *Man*, 7: 4 (1972), 601–13.

ternation of contrasting relational oppositions. Although they counter-balance the collectivizing activities of ritual against the differentiating ones of everyday life, they conceptualize *both* modes of action in oppositional, differentiating terms. It is a culture of mutually opposed oppositions, as it were, a dialectic of sacred and profane or soul and anthropomorphic "power" whose continual expression and rediffer-entiation amounts to nothing more or less than the ongoing inven-tion of society. By continually differentiating each set of oppositional relations from the other, isolating it and protecting it from profanation or contamination, or deliberately activating it so as to negate the other, tribal peoples objectify their conventional orientation of self in rela-tion to the world. They mediate the conventional through the dialectic.

This is why they insist so strongly on the distinctions and boundaries between these modalities, for such differentiation is the very core of their social self-invention. Just as a collective self is invented through the consciously differentiating activities of the individual, so a con-ventional orientation of such a self in relation to a world of "powers" is invented and sustained by the differentiation of "profane" and "sacred" contexts on the part of society at large. By inventing the relations of everyday and ritual activities *against* one another, they counterinvent the totality, the conceptual frame of reference, that in-cludes both of them. The taboos, precautions, and other practices and elements that distinguish "sacred" from "profane" or "secular" stand in the very midst of life because they are the means of social self-invention, and not because tribal peoples are obsessed with a fear of incest, for example, or are the prey of hovering anxieties.

Society in this instance is conceived and operated (from "within") as a set of (differentiating) devices for eliciting consistency and simi-larity, and its most basic distinctions are the ones that "put the world together." Often the same individuals are obliged to play both the "everyday" and the "creative" parts as explicit roles, though on dif-ferent occasions. The Aranda man who ordinarily lives by differ-entiating his role against those of his wife and family must, on certain "ritual" occasions, differentiate himself against society by transforming himself into an *inapertwa* creature, a creative being that shares both human and animal characteristics, and thus permits the ritualist both to increase animal species and to reconstitute his own society. The Daribi man who goes into seclusion and communes with harmful ghosts in the bush during the *habu* ceremony likewise undergoes a transformation from an "everyday" to a "creative" phase of motivation and action, characteristically surrounded by precautions against pro-fanation of the *habu* men by contact with women, and against the *habu* sickness that the ghost inflicts on misusers of the ceremony.

By observing these precautions and distinctions, society creates itself sequentially and episodically as a cosmological harmony, producing a manageable power as well as the social institutions and situations in which that power is applied. Such creativity is by nature cyclical, producing one and then the other aspect of the totality by turns, and it generally falls into a loose rhythm, which may be more or less regular (seasonal, annual, prompted by the cumulative nature of "ordinary" cultural actions), though it may also be broken by crisis or catastrophe. Where it is seasonal, annual, or otherwise linked to phenomenal cycles, as among the periodic "world renewal" ceremonials of North American Indians, or the winter "ceremonial season" on the Northwest Coast, we can say that society objectifies the regularity of natural phenomena through its own order. Otherwise, as with the pig-feasts and exchange cycles of the New Guinea Highlands, the "self-balancing" or "self-motivating" quality of the self-creation stands out in relief; these ceremonies are motivated by such cumulative consequences of ordinary life as pigs proliferating and breaking into gardens and the accumulation of young men who "need initiating." But in both instances the "creative" or ritual mode of action is assumed in order to maintain control over what threatens to become uncontrolled power and carry the world, or men's gardens, or society as a whole, to destruction.

Ritual cycles, distinctions, and precautions define and objectify the conventions of society itself. Those individuals who would attain power and set themselves in a creative role in relation to society must learn to subordinate this self-balancing tendency of society to the will and desires of a "power." They must, in other words, learn to mediate the dialectic through the articulation of the collective, and so must undergo a personal conventional inversion—a shift in identification from soul to power—and a corresponding inversion of actional mode. Such individuals—shamans, sorcerers, healers, witches, and powerful men—come to invent themselves as idiosyncratic powers related to society through the collectivities they create. But the transition to such a state is difficult and dangerous, for the conventional orientation (the self as soul) tends to persist and maintain itself through the production of hysterical symptoms. So the process in which one learns to identify with the power, and thus mediate the dialectic through collectivizing action, involves sickness, self-denial, and the contradiction of convention: a common notion is that the shaman "dies" and "is reborn." If successful the process leads to the exorcism of internal tensions by transforming the inner dialectic into an external one between the individual and society.

Except for occasional ceremonials or interpersonal alliances, such individuals seldom act in concert, much less unite in a guild or pass along their techniques in anything but a personal way. Each stands in a personal dialectical relation to society, established by his own efforts and defined by and large by the idiosyncrasy of his own techniques. If they *did* manage to unite within some conventional or institutional framework, the result would be a transformation of the episodic and cyclical dialectic of social creation into a creative counterpoint of distinct social *classes*. Where such a socially constituted "division of creative labor" does come into being (as it has many times in the course of human history) it amounts to an innovation on the form of tribal culture, a distinct and different invention of society. The component classes in this kind of dialectic stand in a relationship of mutual and simultaneous creativity to one another; they divide the worlds of invention and convention between them.

But the conditions under which such a class division comes into being effectively rule out any awareness of this dialectical relationship among those who are engaged in inventing society. For the change from an alternating and episodic creativity to a static relation between social classes places the responsibility for creating and sustaining the conventional aspect of culture (its distinction between innate and artificial) upon one of the subdivisions of society. Thus the differentiation (distinctions and precautions separating "sacred" and "profane") by which society invents itself as a conscious dialectic of one mode of creativity versus the other, is replaced by the collectivizing efforts of a single social segment. At the inception of an urban civilization, *the mediation of conventional forms through the dialectic gives way to a mediation of dialectical relations through the articulation of conventionalized contexts.* The balance has been tipped: what Jakobson, Lévi-Strauss, and Barthes refer to as "paradigmatic" thought has yielded to what they call "syntagmatic"—society invents itself as the articulation of a principle rather than as the dialectical interaction of principles.

The implications of this are momentous and far-reaching. The mediation of dialectical change via collectivizing action introduces a profound disharmony between the conceptualization of action and its effects. Although the (differentiating versus collectivizing) controls used respectively by the two "classes" or subdivisions of society stand in a dialectical relationship to one another, this relationship (and the corresponding interaction of the classes) is continually expressed and reinvented in nondialectical form. It is perceived and constituted as the linear organization of society as a whole in relation to God or in relation to nature. And by thus ignoring its own internal dialectic society loses the ability to maintain its conventional orientation of

the self to the world, and of what is "given" and innate to what results from human action. There is nothing to check the progressive
differentiation of the conventionalized controls or the progressive collectivization of nonconventionalized controls. An ongoing "relativization" of this sort becomes an inevitable part of social action. Instead
of motivating itself *dialectically,* society does so *historically.* Instead of
affording a solution, its internal dynamic poses the major problem.

A society that undertakes to mediate dialectical change through the
articulation of conventionalized contexts dooms itself to the percepion
and attempted solution of what are basically social problems in non-
social terms. The ideological and practical "solution" invariably
creates unmanageable problems, and these problems invariably concern the relations between "classes" or segments of society. Such an
enterprise begins as an attempt to invent society as the hierarchical
relationship of man to the anthropomorphic powers (the Church,
theocratic city-states, holy empires)—a creation by certain classes of the
collective as "god" and "soul." But the conventionalized controls used
in this invention become increasingly differentiated (God turns into
saints, saints become relics, the Church is a mass of orders, universal
offices become worldly fiefs), motivating the devout to ever more
energetic efforts at purgation, reformation, and conversion. At the
same time the tasks and roles of "everyday" life become increasingly
collectivized (facilitating, and facilitated by, the use of money in exchange) and assimilated to a common "Culture." Eventually the
"given" loses its collective and anthropomorphic nature and is differentiated into a world of natural phenomena, whereas man's activities become the collective center of his life. Culture gradually
secularizes and democratizes itself, inverting its concept of self and its
orientation of self to world; the attempt to invent society as man's
relation to divinity leads to the rise of the bourgeoisie.

This is no solution. For the attempt to invent society as man's
rational and scientific relation to nature is merely another way of
mediating the dialectic through the conventional. The conventionalized controls of a Culture of collective enterprise are gradually differentiated into discrete specializations and life styles; workers organize
into unions, and the populace becomes a collection of "minorities."
Simultaneously the disparate contexts of the world of nature come to
be ordered and collectivized, so that nature takes on an increasingly
sociomorphic—and even anthropomorphic—form. Just as the cumulative differentiation of the divine and collectivization of the secular
motivated the leaders of medieval times to restore the collectivity of
the sacred by insisting on social distinctions, so the men and women
of the modern world are moved to do justice to natural discreteness

(individual, racial, and so on) by integrating and organizing society. But their efforts can only lead to greater differentation, even as the differentiating efforts of their forebears led to the rise of the bourgeoisie. The only real solution can come about through a growth of social consciousness to the point where the separate classes or segments of society are able to interact and create one another in a conscious dialectic. This corresponds to a second "inversion" of cultural orientation, in which the conventions of society as a whole are mediated by a dialectic between classes.

Thus the attempt to mediate the dialectic through the articulation of the collective produces the same consequences for a culture as a whole as the attempt to do this on a personal scales does for the shaman in tribal society. It leads to an inversion of experience and identification as a necessary stage in the development of a social dialectic. On a cultural scale this process generates widespread mass motivations and efforts at expansion: the Crusades, the Reformation, the world wars, and colonialism are examples. It amounts to the phemomenon that we think of as the rise of urban civilization.

The rise of civilizations

Since we began our discussion of cultural invention with an exploration of the dialectical creation of meaning, it is necessary at this point to ask what happens when such a dialectic is "mediated." Does this mean that the dialectic ceases to operate? Scarcely, for we have seen that the relations necessary to meaning itself are dialectical in form, opposing the collective to the individual and particular. Mediation of the dialectic simply makes its expression and operation dependent upon nondialectical means. A cultural tradition that mediates the dialectic through collectivizing relations and expressions learns to create and understand a basically dialectical world in linear and rational terms. It builds an ideological world out of "one-way," causal connections, denying and deemphasizing the contradictory, paradoxical, and reciprocal aspects of man's thought and culture.

We need not go far to find examples of this style of thought and action, for we have encountered them over and over again in our examination of modern American Culture. The ideology that links God and country, and the commonplace saying that religion and science are not really irreconcilable are cases in point. So is the advertiser's claim that he is simply passing on "information" about his product. In his own mind the advertiser does not want to individuate his brand so much as make its name and characteristics a household word—part of the collective technology and life of the culture. The political candidate likewise develops his "image" and his platform against those of his opponents because he wants to make his own views those of the "administration." Americans differentiate *in the interests of collectivizing.* This is what we mean by "competition." Differentiation and contradiction are rationalized and "worked into the system" as "means" to a single, monolithic "end"—a better life, a more democratic administration, a sounder species, and so forth.

The dialectic is always "there." It is just being "used" differently in this kind of situation. The inherent contradictions and paradoxes it embodies are "masked" in the collectivizing objectifications used to mediate it. This is why advertising, entertainment, the "media," and popular religion do not admit to their status as an "interpretive culture"; they must "mask" the creative and contradictory nature of their efforts by justifying them as contributions to a collective whole. They are part of a tradition that invents itself as man's relation to nature, rather than the creative relationship of one part of society to the other. The history of such a tradition is riddled with examples of dialectical contradiction: bishops and popes with mistresses and families, executives and politicians who machinate to "make things come out right," scientists who "finagle" their methodologies—all with rationalizations to justify their actions. This is a mode of cultural action that *uses* the dialectic rather than embodies it, though because it uses the dialectic it is in turn used by it, turning cultural effort into a self-motivating development.

How does this mode of action come about? The historian Oswald Spengler suggests that there is something in the *content* of the collectivities articulated in the development of a civilization that demands articulation. He calls this the culture's *ursymbol,* or "prime symbol," an elemental perception of spatio-temporal extension that gives the art, architecture, literature, religion, science, philosophy, and mathematics of a civilization its specific form. In his *The Decline of the West,*[6] he develops a thesis of the basic morphological similarity of developmental phases in all nascent civilizations by contrasting the conceptual contents of different ones.

Nor is it unlikely that the conceptual contents of these various high cultures contrast in the ways Spengler has described. Spengler's tendency, however, is to identify so completely with the *ursymbol* and its articulation that he views its termination, the end of a developmental phase, as a kind of negation. Hence the title of his book, and

6. Oswald Spengler, *Der Untergang Des Abendlandes: Umrisse Einer Morphologie Der Weltgeschichte* (Munich: C. H. Beck, 1923).

the profound distress it has caused rationalist historians and disciples of "progress" in the last fifty years. Indeed, the more common idea that "high" cultural development has a "cyclical" morphology has also put these people on the defensive, though I have tried to show that it can be derived through an approach very different from Spengler's. I have suggested that what we call the development of civilization is a self-motivating transition from an episodic to a social power relation, regardless of the symbolic content of its controls. The subject of this discussion is that of how people create their own realities, and how they create themselves and their societies *through* them, rather than the questions of what those realities are, how they originate, or how they relate to what is "really" there.

Whenever a society composed of classes or segments standing in a dialectical relationship to one another, however this may come about, attempts to mediate that relationship through a linear, nondialectical ideology, a disharmony is set up that works to resolve itself. The resolution is self-motivating, whether it takes the short-term form of "cargo cults" raised against the imposition of alien ideas or the long-term form of the inversional development of a nascent civilization. The motivation derives from the fact that whereas each of the societal segments "does" the self and embodies the controls of the members of the other, they act at cross-purposes. Because they have different aims, each perceives the actions of the other as motivational "resistance," spurring it on to greater efforts. And so, instead of creating each other, as societal segments do in a balanced social dialectic, they motivate one another. And because the effects of this mutual motivation overbalance whatever mutual creation *does* take place (between lord and vassal, priest and laity, or advertiser and consumer, for instance), there is nothing to check the progressive relativization of the controls.

Consider the situation in medieval Europe. The clergy and nobility created their personal individuality and their distinctness as hierarchical classes through the objectification of society as man's collective relationship to God. Their controls in this enterprise were the conventionalized ones of religious doctrine and formulae, embracing other codes, such as feudal law, as well. The peasantry created man's communality in substance and in spirit through living particular life styles and occupational specialties. Their controls were the differentiating ones of male or female work, or of particular craft techniques, or specialized functions. Each segment of society "did" the self, and embodied the work, of the other, and because fundamental interests were opposed, each motivated the other to a more or less continuous application and reapplication of its controls.

The individual "selves" of the nobility and clergy were continually subject to the threat of profanation and loss of hierarchical status through the emulation of peasant "worldliness." But the collective self of the peasant or artisan was likewise subject to regimentation and manipulation in the name of its own salvation, which threatened his free action. Thus each segment of society was motivated to use its collectivizing or differentiating controls in counteracting the "resistance" embodied in the actions of the other. The secular problems and situations posed by the peasants and artisans *differentiated* the conventionalized controls of religious formula and doctrine and feudal code, causing them to be "broken down" into specific instances. But the more fragmented and differentiated these became, the greater the challenge to the rulers and clergy to overcome them by collectivizing— a redoubled effort at applying the controls which could only lead, paradoxically, to further differentiation. Simultaneously these efforts at centralizing and regimentation had the effect of *collectivizing* the controls of secular life, welding them into a complementary whole whose equating measure was money and whose locus was the town. The more those caught up in secular life sought to flee the taxation and regimentation that such collectivization implied, by building "new towns" or seeking charters for "free cities," the more they aided the collectivization of their controls.

Differentiation drove a wedge between nobility and clergy, elements of the "collectivizing" aspect of society whose power and aspirations had coincided under the emperors Charlemagne and Otto I. At the same time it fragmented and particularized the spheres of both elements. The feudal bond had originally been a pledge of total commitment and support between lord and vassal, grounded in honor.[7] But gradually, through the extension of feudal forms to cover more and more diverse situations, the fiefs and services exchanged became increasingly particularized: for example a cup of wine for watch duty on Christmas Eve. In addition, vassals came to have more than one lord; the bond lost its totality of commitment. The concept of *liege homage* was developed to correct this, the liegeman being the one lord to whom a vassal's chief duty lay. But, as Bloch observes, ". . . precisely because liege homage was merely the resurrection of the primitive form of homage, it was bound in its turn to be affected by the same causes of decline."[8] Men came to have more than one liege lord.

7. See Max Weber, *Wirtschaft und Gesellschaft,* 1 (Tübingen: J. C. B. Mohr, 1965), p. 148; and also F. L. Ganshof, *Feudalism,* tr. Philip Grierson (London: Longmans, Green and Co., 1952), p. xv.

8. Marc Bloch, *Feudal Society,* tr. L. A. Manyon (Chicago: University of Chicago Press, 1961), p. 216.

Religious doctrine and the Church were also differentiated and particularized at all levels. Doctrine proliferated into different points of view and heresies (which both Abelard and Aquinas attempted to deal with), its Godhead into particular saints and other mediating functionaries, and these in turn became particularized in the form of specific visions, shrines, and relics. Just as fiefs and services became diversified, so men's sins and the corresponding penances were classified, enumerated, added to—good and evil came to be very complex. The Church's organizational form particularized itself into separate orders (among them the Hospitallers and Templers, the Teutonic Order, the Franciscans and Dominicans) and into landed and endowed bishoprics and abbeys, rights and privileges.

The tasks and roles of secular life became increasingly interdependent, so that as the conventionalized controls of medieval life gradually lost their coherence in a growing relativization, social institutions began to rely more and more upon the collectivizing forms of secular life. The granting of fiefs was replaced by a money payment (the *fief-rente*), and the services of vassals were commuted to a return payment (*scutage*) to finance the wars and domestic dealings of the lord or king. The traders and artisans in the towns began to borrow the collectivizing forms of the rulers, founding guilds (each with its patron saint), town organizations, and finally even leagues of towns, as among those of the Lombard League in Italy or the towns of the Rhineland.

Often, and with increasing frequency, as we pass from the fourteenth to the sixteenth centuries, the mutual motivation of the two segments of society (by now each diversified into numerous "classes") was experienced as exploitation. Instead of "making one do" one's differentiating or collectivizing tasks, the actions of the other part of society were as "something being done" to one, causing an inversion of controls in an effort to deal with the impinging force. Peasants and townsmen rose in rebellion and sought to take control of the Church or state; there were the peasant rebellion of Wat Tyler in England, the later and bloodier rebellions in Germany, Savonarola in Italy, and Jan Hus in Bohemia. The nobility and clergy were driven again and again to maintain the integrity of state or religion through acts of differentiation. They granted codes or charters to particular regions or cities and founded new and "purified" monastic orders or religious creeds.

The culmination of these efforts took the form of a massive and protracted inversion of cultural controls, identifiable with such historical phenomena as the Reformation, the religious wars, and the birth and rise of empirical science. What had been the uniting and collectivizing controls of Latin Christendom became personalizing and differentiating, and what had formerly served to differentiate the sexes and roles of secular life became a consciously collectivizing Culture. The breakdown of religion into "denominations," Luther's proclamation of a faith based on conscience, Calvin's religious community in Geneva and his followers' doctrine of personal predestination, Henry VIII's formation of the Church of England, and the appearance of national monarchies were all catalyzing events in this inversion. It would be a mistake to limit the process of inversion to such events, for in an important sense it began with the rise of the bourgeoisie in Lombardy and the Rhineland in the 1100s and persisted through to the Scopes "monkey trial" in our century. Yet in most respects the Culture of collective enterprise that forms a basis for our society and our science came into being in the Europe of the fifteenth, sixteenth, and seventeenth centuries.

In this respect the discoveries of Copernicus, Galileo, Kepler, Newton, and the other "creators" of the early modern world were not so much new additions to our store of "knowledge" as they were precedents for a new kind of invention of self in relation to world. In their seeking for the "celestial harmonies" of the medieval imagination, these men encountered, and taught others to discover and experience, a new kind of cosmos, a particularized nature of diverse events and regularities not easily derivable from those of human society. Man came to embody, and to live in a world of natural diversity, united by his own efforts to master and understand it.

The collective aspect of society was henceforth increasingly invented by the urban, moneyed bourgeoisie, and the forms of bourgeois thought and action were used to mediate the dialectic between the classes. At first, roughly until the French Revolution, the chief motivating interaction occurred between the bourgeoisie and the "upper classes" of nobility and clergy. The consciously collectivizing efforts of the middle class, which triumphed in the Netherlands' Republic and in Cromwell's England, was otherwise carried on against the motivating "resistance" of an absolutist territorial nobility and a sectarian clergy. The nation-state was "defended" (differentiated, kept distinct from others) and defined in character by its upper classes, and united and maintained economically (collectivized) by the bourgeoisie. Nobility and clergy created the standards of personal comportment (refinement, breeding, leisure) and moral conscience, whereas the bourgeoisie defined (in its controls of money and practicality) the standards of purpose and achievement for the whole.

But the "motivating" effects of nobility and clergy upon the dominant collectivizing ideology made their position of leadership and authority increasingly precarious. A culture that lived by the standards of money and rationality was increasingly moved to rule itself by these standards. So, beginning with the American and French revolutions, and continuing through a period of struggle, colonialism, and revolution in the nineteenth and early twentieth centuries, rationalistic and bourgeois forms of thought and government (democracy and science) replaced those of authoritarian individuation. It was a transition that took place as much within the personality as within the social, economic, and intellectual organization of society. Freud's "miraculous" cures of hysterics and his less successful attempts to cope with neurosis (including his own) suggests that his therapy consisted of the conversion of his patients to rationalism. Psychoanalysis can be seen as a "fieldwork" experience of re-creating a "normal" (i.e., "responsible") personality by exorcising the guilty dialectic of personal history. David Riesman's work has demonstrated the gradual replacement of "inner directed" (consciously differentiating) by "other directed" (consciously collectivizing) styles of work, consumption, and socialization in the emergence of modern American society.

Thus we arrive at the self-creation and self-motivation of modern Western Culture. Like other attempts at mediating the dialectic through the articulation of the conventional, it is inherently unstable; the collectivizing solutions that it believes in and contrives with an ever increasing sense of urgency only serve to create the "given" world of individual fact and incident in a more demanding form. Society is challenged by its very creations: the "stubborn facts" of history and science, the pressing "needs" of ethnic and regional "minorities," the "crises" that develop out of existing differences and points of view. All have the effect of differentiating and ultimately deconventionalizing our collectivizing controls. By attempting to "integrate" and satisfy minorities, we create them; by trying to "explain" and universalize facts and events we fragment our theories and categories; by applying universal theories naively to the study of cultures we invent those cultures as stubborn and inviolable individualities. Each failure motivates a greater collectivizing effort.

The effect of this process is to force a greater and greater reliance upon dialectical means. Advertising, journalism, and other forms of "mass culture" become inevitable. The necessity of keeping up the forms and appearances of a rational and democratic Culture through informal and ad hoc means forces politicians, executives, scientists, and others into the "double bind" of cultural "illegitimacy," in their own eyes as well as others'. The only solution lies in the general legitimation and acceptance of consciously dialectical forms of thought and action. The existence of civilized traditions with long-established patterns of dialectical social integration suggests that the transition to such inherently stable forms has been made many times in human history. The scholars, Brahmins, rabbis, mullahs, and "enlightened" teachers of Chinese, Hindu, Judaic, and Islamic society, and of many Buddhist sects and societies, live in a dialectical balance (sometimes very complex, as in India) with other elements of the social whole. This does not mean that these societies are "perfect" or "without history," or that they are in possession of some supernal or absolute "truth." It simply means that they have a stable structure, one that does not work against itself.

It would be interesting and profitable to explore the potential for this kind of resolution in present-day Western society. But we are concerned with anthropology, and with its peculiar and self-motivating relation to its subject matter. In outlining the modern Western invention of society, we return once again to the problem posed at the beginning of our inquiry, that of the "wax museum," for our anthropology is necessarily a part of our self-invention. It is because our tradition of thought emphasizes the "masking" of dialectical relations through collectivizing action that our self-image of Culture has come to be applied indiscriminately to the lifeways of others. There is a certain motivated necessity in our tendency to lump all human cultures together as a single evolutionary effort. It is an act of justification for our own invention of society as man's relation to nature. As long as anthropology strives to mediate its relationship with its subject peoples as part of something else, as part of its cultural invention of "reality," rather than dialectically, it will need the "primitive." It will remain fascinated with what it regards as "natural" and elemental, and misconstrue the intentions and expression of other forms of human existence in terms of its own values, as an "allegory of man."

chapter 6

The invention of anthropology

The allegory of man

As is the case with "culture," our use of the word "human" embodies a very strategic ambiguity. It is both an identification of ourselves as a species and the expression of a moral ideal. Just as "culture" links a peculiarly Western and rationalistic assessment of our achievements with a much more general phenomenon, so "human" coordinates a "natural" and biological phenomenon with a set of moral assumptions. A human being emerges as a life form with certain capacities; its "humanity" is the degree to which it lives up to those capacities. Thus "becoming human" in our tradition is a moral task for the individual as well as an evolutionary one for the species, and the resolution to treat these two aspects as the same thing has given our study of man's origins its teleological and moralistic overtones. Conversely, the biological image of man is imbued with moral attributes so specific that they ought in all frankness to be referred to particular instances of "culture" or dismissed as "projections."

Insofar as it has come to rely upon the paradigm of man versus nature as a central insight, our study of man's origins has assumed the significance of an allegory of man, a simulation of past human development through the moral terms of "being human." The point of contrast throughout is "nature," understood as an a priori source and fount of energy and substance, located within the individual (in the manner of an "id," or libidinal force) as well as outside of him. The attainment of "humanity" is understood as the refinement and application of this supreme "given" through the creation of order, to produce the phenomena of the "tempered" personality and of "artificial" cultural action. "Humanity" is thus nature refined and drawn through the meshes of a conscious purpose and order, a discipline that is itself objectified as something that can be learned, taught, preserved, recorded, and extended. This order is the "state" of philosophers like Locke and Rousseau, the "culture" of the later evolutionary anthropologists, and the "progress" of modern simplifiers.

If the allegory of man's "becoming human" is to be realized as an evolutionary sequence, it must have a beginning. Hence the myth of "natural man" is born; an unrefined man, as it were, all "instinct" and impulse. The notion of man "without culture" is generally disavowed today, and even Rousseau doubtless intended his "noble savage" as a heuristic construct, but "natural man" (or thinly disguised equivalents) crops up in discussions again and again with a resiliency that suggests some profound necessity for our way of thinking. Indeed, we are all made to "feel" natural man within us, as the impulsive "animal" that propels wondrous instincts like hunger, sex, and aggression. But for an age that has been taught, by Wynne-Edwards and others, to perceive the significantly "cultural" essence of most animal life styles, the genealogical locus, and in fact the very possibility, of such an intuitive "animal-man" becomes a matter of greater and greater dubiousness. If we cannot find an uncultured animal, in other words, if wolves treat one another with the tempered gentility of rococo courtiers, and tigers kill for the abandoned young of other carnivores, why single out man's forebears as the only real beasts in the zoo? Rousseau, at least, thought nature benign, and later generations could content themselves with the blanket term "instinct," but our own generation is coming to realize that this concept can be applied to practically everything—and therefore explains nothing.[1]

Man has always been cultural, just as he has always been natural. It is extremely unlikely that he was ever generally crude, brutish, slovenly, or unsophisticated. Crude, unsophisticated animals do not

---

1. The question of instinctive versus learned (nature versus nurture) ultimately devolves into the same *cul-de-sac* as that of "natural" versus "psychosomatic" illness. For a superb discussion, see Gregory Bateson's "Metalogue: What is an Instinct?" in *Approaches to Animal Communication,* ed. Thomas A. Sebeok (The Hague: Mouton, 1969).

survive very well. In fact it is the very competence and sophistication that every ancestral form of man must undoubtedly have had (if he was to be anybody's ancestor at all) that calls the standard utilitarian explanations of man's cultural development most into doubt. The principle of natural selection requires that a strong adaptive pressure must bear upon any given species throughout its evolutionary history; there is no place for the luxury of crudeness or the preservation of an inept race that may one day accomplish great things. It is not too difficult to imagine how a "favorable" genetic change can gain an evolutionary foothold, but virtually impossible to understand why members of a sophisticated, "well-adapted" culture should want to change its well-proven ways in favor of some "practical" improvement whose "benefits" contradict their values. A social or technological "improvement," after all, achieves its obvious utilitarian value only after it has been established long enough and well enough for there to be a "need" for it.

Of course the utilitarian advantages (or disadvantages!) of such changes do eventually show up, though it would be foolish to attribute these consequences to the motives of the original inventors, who must certainly have valued their creations for their impact on a different, earlier set of circumstances. Like all other innovations they conjure power through the novel and strategic ways in which they impinge upon the "given," and the effects they may have had for mankind are contingent and secondary, whether or not these occurred to the inventors. Whether it is accomplished by "accident" and interpretation or by plan, invention has the initial effect (and outright significance) of power. The attempt to attribute moral motives and utilitarian foresight to the conjurers of this power, to explain events and justify actions on the basis of what was to them an unknowable future, is as much an example of allegorical thinking as the illusion of "natural man." It projects our concept of "Culture" as a public, purposeful, and externally created moral order upon acts and incidents whose only common denominator can have been a certain innovative force; its social and moral interests reduce creativity to practicality.

If we are to understand man's origins and his phenomenal existence, we must examine his creativity as it manifests itself at every point in his ongoing cultural life, and not merely in retrospect. To be sure, many of yesterday's innovations become part of tomorrow's transmitted "culture," whether this involves their assimilation to the allegedly "innate" social roles of peasant and tribal societies, or the consciously fabricated Cultures of man's urban civilizations. Yet for all our own recognition of this fact, it is doubly important for us to realize that in their assimilation to a permanent tradition, these elements become the basis for further innovations. Their behavioral, demographic, ecological, and social effects are themselves inextricably bound up with the ongoing exercise of creativity, of continuous innovation, that is culture; their very "transmission" and "reception" are to an important degree a kind of inventive "induction." A great invention is "reinvented" many times and in many circumstances as it is taught, learned, used, and improved, often in combination with other inventions.

Because they are now the property of society—indeed, they are *properties* of the social and moral order—ideology would have us apprehend and appreciate these assimilated inventions (and their origins) within the accepted context. It stresses their necessary relation to the present social existence and its goals and can, when required, develop a likely "origin" for any one of them by objectifying this relation in terms of primeval situations. Hence the utilitarian and teleological nature of much of our conjecture about man's past. Moreover, since ideology must perforce mask its operations in terms of the "magical" efficacy of the gods, rituals, or technologies themselves, the inceptions of its major components are always represented as phenomena sui generis. They are "accidental," "bolts from the blue," the inexplicable attainments of a great genius, the gift of a god who appeared in a vision, rather than particularly striking manifestations of that wonderfully inventive and imaginative being whose creative ramblings keep our psychiatrists occupied, stock the shelves of our inflated fiction industry to overflowing, and inundate patent offices with the bastard broods of Mother Necessity.

This insistence on the *randomness* of invention is merely the other side of the coin of social interest; an ideology that allegorizes its own origins through present goals and interrelationships would *have* to represent its early discoveries as sui generis occurrences, since the relational aspects that it would stress (the "needs" by which it excuses their adoption and retention) were not in existence at the time of their discovery. Once fire has been tamed, for whatever mad motive, by whatever very clever ("very gifted," "very lucky") inventor, with whatever profound spiritual revelations or strategic effects, someone is eventually (who knows how much later?) going to use it for light, for heat, for cremating or making toast, and thus integrate it into its "proper" role. (*We* do not use fire so much for personal companionship or as a social center, and so tend to ignore these otherwise perfectly "adaptational" and "practical" roles.) Our habit of allegory traps us into imagining that fire meant the same thing to everyone, including its first domesticators, that it means to us.

Thus in all its particulars the allegory of man represents a racial phylogeny in the terms of our culture's idealized ontogeny. Just as the individual develops and refines his "natural" gifts and talents, his "native intelligence," through the artificial, learnable, and perfectable moral order of society, so the animalistic "natural man" adapts and improves himself, evolves, through the creation and extension of culture (tool-making). Technology, man's collective, transmittable, effective, and adaptive effort, is the subject of this evolution, and the refinement and improvement of his physical characteristics (his "natural endowments") is its object. Man "himself," his overt physical constitution, with its implications of innate ability such as "intelligence" (cranial capacity and conformation), manipulative dexterity, (posture, hands, jaws), and general "humanness," is the ostensible manifestation of a kind of progress. But since the beginning point of this developmental epic is allegedly some sort of ("uncultured") animal-man, and its conclusion is modern (urban, educated) man, our interpretive efforts run a grave risk of degenerating into a phrenology of brow ridges, foreheads, and cranial vaults, a fetishism of "primitive" and "animal-like" as opposed to "progressive" and "man-like" details.

Man is of course no less "natural," no less of an animal, now than he has ever been. He is no more "cultural" in his present state than his forebears were. The physical evidence that we possess for his evolution indicates a variety of forms (whose respective "cultural" capacities are, to put it mildly, difficult to determine) that seem to have diminished in number, and the eventual preponderance of modern-looking types. (Though for all we can tell homo erectus—a contemporary of homo sapiens over much of his existential span—was just as well suited to "bear" human culture as his more notable colleague.) If we dismiss the allegories of animals turning into men, of "missing links" and hopeful apes, we are left with the conclusion that human evolution amounts to the intensification of certain proclivities of man as a form of life, and an expression of this intensification in all the particulars of man's life.

There are good reasons for making this suggestion. First of all, as Geertz and others have pointed out in recent years, man's physical being and his "cultural" attributes have evolved together, evolved *through* each other, so to speak. His tools shaped him even as he shaped them. But more important even than this long-term adaptation to culture itself is the fact that man's self-creation is constant and complete. Not only does he adapt to the culture he creates, but he uses that external creation as a control in the forging of his own aggressions, desires, and impulses; much of the "innate," too, is created in the same transient, repetitive, and stylistically conditioned way that arrowheads, meals, and festivals are created. Man's constitutional and behavioral nature is not simply the rather lethargic teammate of his purposeful creation, his "culture"; its involvement is both more immediate and more complex than that.

To put the matter somewhat differently, the "culture" through which man's present physical constitution has come into its own incorporates both controls on his self-invention, the conscious and the unconscious ones. It is not only tools, house types, paintings, costume, and ceremonial, but also fear, anger, aggression, and desire, and the latter are quite as "artificial" (and as "natural") as the former. The physical constitution is not separable from the thing we call "culture," even as part of a dialectic; it can rather be distinguished as an arbitrary "level" for the description of phenomena. If man has "changed" over the past few hundred millennia, if his invention and possession of "self" has increased in control through the gain in control over his external creativity (and vice versa), then nature itself has changed quite as much as man; we have not "diverged" from nature at all.

Man is a mediator of things, a kind of universal catalyst. In his mind's eye he is a builder, a purposeful actor and shaper of nature, or else a sympathetic partner and collaborator with the world's "powers." But he is also able, in the most elemental sense, to make himself permeable to things, to "become" in his thoughts, identifications, and imaginings, the things around him, to make them a part of his knowing, acting, and being. The modality of meaningful intention and action that we have called "control" is effective only to the degree that the actor accepts this permeability, this "becoming," as "real." Man lives through the things around him, lives in a world in which they and their qualities are real. He is, as Rilke once suggested, the form of their transformation, and all his faith, hope, patience, expectation, and belief in life and the purpose of his action are invested in the understanding that these transformations are actual accomplishments—that the verification of science is absolute, that the wine and the wafer become Christ. And yet, possessed as he is by these impersonations, by these things in the form of thoughts and thoughts in the form of things, man can only realize his own social and individual self by his failure to live up to them. His "humanity" is always inadvertent, an increment of living through other people and things and letting them live through him.

Or, to phrase it perhaps more accurately, man lives through ideas, people, and things *at the expense* of their living through him. Every significant innovation in man's life style has had the effect of increasing his dependency as well as the "energy" and degree of technical or social "leverage" at his disposal. This is the price of involvement, and man's peculiar adaptation, that of a mediator, is nothing if not a program of increasingly intensive involvement: man's material and spiritual sustenance amounts to the kind of gain realized by an organism that is part of a symbiosis. In fact, humanity multiplies this basic factor of interdependence through the whole range of its operations. The mind is constrained by its "languages," by the imagery of controls through which it knows and expresses itself; the nomadic herdsman is a slave to the sheep that feed him, peasantries are "rooted" in the soil, and the present generation is beginning to realize the tragic implications of that most significant consequence of "Culture" as accumulation, the city.

The problem of defining man as a phenomenon, of deciding what he "is," is the problem of presenting the essential personality of a very clever and elusive masquerade and disguise artist in the guise of one of his masks. Man is so many things, one is tempted to introduce him in a particularly bizarre get-up just to show what he can do, or at least choose a disguise that will reinforce a special line of argument. And yet everything that he is he also is not, so his more constant nature is not one of being but of becoming. Even the conceit that he must be a consummate masquerader is only true in this sense, since the actor or masquerader can only succeed in his performance by denying that it is a mere "act," and hence a successful masquerader is one who is able to "be" what he is not by being what he is.

The thing that makes man so interesting as a phenomenon is that he is precisely *not* what simplifiers have made him out to be. He is neither a carnivore nor a herbivore, neither killer ape nor naked ape, as much made by tools as he is a tool maker, as much the tool of language as language is his tool. He is all of these things, and therefore none of them; the metaphor for his striking mode of being, for his metaphoric mode of being, has eluded scientist and interpreter alike. If he were simply a killer or a lamb of the pastures, simply a computer or an "equilibrium state," it would not have been necessary to write this (or any other) book about him: indeed, man would scarcely find it necessary either to write books or to read them.

As allegories of an emergent humanity, the metaphors selected to articulate our expectations of man's evolution ("ape-man," "erect, socializing primate," "tool maker") feature the same ideological components as do our moral and psychological models: the innate ("natural") and the artificial ("cultural"). They exploit a particular ideological position, that of man's self-improvement and self-constraint through the creation of an artificial "rational" order, as a source of insight into his origins and essence. Yet what is arbitrary and imposed is not man's culture alone, which, like his physical being, is as much natural as it is consciously created, but the distinction between nature and culture. This distinction is the artifact (and the essence) of our ideology, and for that reason imprisons any intellectual enterprise that subscribes to it within the confines of our self-imposed way of thinking. There is not, nor was there ever, an exclusively "natural" man or an exclusively "artificial" culture.

The problem to which evolutionary anthropology addresses itself becomes the tautology: "How did a natural order conceivable in cultural terms transform itself into a humanity conceptualized in natural terms?" "Cultural evolution" refers to the way in which the sociomorphic tendencies that we believe to be "implicit" in nature (and that we *put* into nature through our acts of explanation) turn into explicit "rules" of a functioning society. It is the history of legitimation (the social contract, in which "natural man's" inclinations became Culture) or of human "cognition" (man's existence as a scientific or folk-scientific discovery of the phenomenal world). But in fact this evolutionary viewpoint is simply an inversion, like a movie run backward, of the subliminal invention of self and of the natural proclivity that accompanies our everyday life. We create nature, and tell ourselves stories about how nature creates us!

Controlling culture

The serious business of modern American Culture is that of taming, harnessing, subduing, tempering, rationalizing, and understanding the powerful and mystifying thing that we believe to be within us and around us, and to animate all things—which we call "nature." Our personal and collective values are all measured by this enterprise, whether we speak of health, sanity, performance, sportsmanship, morality, or progress. Our collective Culture is a vast accumulation of material and spiritual achievements and resources stemming from the conquest of nature and necessary to the continuance of this effort. It includes the substantial foundations of our cities and economic life, the massive banks of "information" and "knowledge" that fill our libraries and computers, the triumphs of art and science, and the arcane and ubiquitous labyrinths of technology. These are our heritage, our property, our life and our work, and our means of carrying forth our ideals and commitments.

But I have argued that this whole vast complex amounts to a highly articulated and ever-changing set of controls for the invention of nature through acts of objectification. Since a belief in the "reality" of that which is invented is a necessary part of objectification, however, it follows that the effects of these controls are "masked" and concealed from those who use them. Thus the ideology of American culture is based on the existence of a phenomenal and innate order called "nature" as distinct from the artificial and perfectable thing we call "culture." Instead of inventing nature, we are said to understand it, harness it, apply it, let it take its course. All of our dealings with the phenomenal world, whether speculative or practical, respect the primacy and innateness of nature and natural force.

This gives a tremendous power and advantage to those who have the job of interpreting nature, natural force, impulse, or event. For they possess, or at least claim, the authority to determine what nature is like in all its "innate" forms, and they therefore become the arbiters of Culture. If the whole of Culture attains its importance and value through the tempering and application of nature, then an assertion of what the facts of nature *are* stands as an evaluation of Culture. Scientists and medical men (who interpret the nature within us and around us), entertainers (who interpret emotion and "innate" reaction), advertisers (who interpret impulse and need), and journalists (who interpret events and their importance) stand in a power relation to culture. They objectify Culture through the "innate," differentiating its forms (and thereby recharging and creating them) through a vast number of nonconventionalized controls.

Americans are vulnerable to this kind of manipulation because their belief in the reality of the nature invented through their Cultural controls is grounded in a conviction based on experience. Nature is an *experience* of something happening to our controls, it is perceived through their objectification. It is felt as the individual self, a peculiar ("motivating") resistance encountered in the effort to "control" or discipline the self; as the force of "natural law" (combustion, electricity, compression) operating in an automobile engine or a household appliance; or as the performance and reactions of the subject in a scientific experiment. And the creativity of the inventor or the designer of a scientific experiment is that of contriving an arrangement of cultural controls (technological devices, experimental situations) that will permit some new way of "using" or "experiencing" (i.e., inventing) nature. In the act of applying or "interrogating" nature, inventing it, we bring into being new cultural controls that can be used by others to re-create the experience again and again. We objectify Culture through the conscious interpretation of nature. Our conscious Culture is a well-articulated accumulation of such created and objectified controls, which can be used again and again to re-create the original experience of nature.

Naturalistic empiricism, the appeal to natural "fact" and the experience of nature as a means of scientific "proof" and certainty, is therefore basically an appeal to the effectiveness of our own cultural controls. It uses the experience of nature that is produced through the application of those controls as a means to justify and extend them. And so it forms the foundation of "straight" or ideologically acceptable science, the creative use of the "given" or "innate" part of our total conception of things for the corroboration and extension of the "artificial" and humanly adjustable part. Because it is based on our ideological distinction specifying which things, and which *kinds* of things, are "given," innate, and unchangeable, and which are not, as an unquestioned article of faith, its rules, procedures, techniques, and methodologies are devices for the reassertion and reinvention of this distinction and the ideology that corresponds to it. And because naturalistic science is therefore always a means of reinforcing and reapplying this distinction, its application is always part of the invention of *our own* culture.

When this kind of approach is turned to the uses of anthropological investigation, it makes our understanding and invention of other cultures dependent upon our own orientation toward "reality," and it makes anthropology into a tool of our own self-invention. Whenever one "aspect" or part of a dialectical and self-creating whole is used as a conscious control in this way, its use must inevitably result in the invention of the other part. When we use the nonconventionalized and differentiating controls of nature in this way, we objectify and re-create our collective Culture with its central ideology of the "natural" versus the "cultural" and artificial. When we use these controls in the study of other peoples we invent their cultures as analogues not of our *whole* cultural and conceptual scheme but of *part* of it. We invent them as analogues of Culture (as "rules," "norms," "grammars," "technologies"), the conscious, collective, "artificial" part of our world, in relation to a single, universal, natural "reality." Thus they do not contrast with our culture, or offer counter-examples to it, as a total system of conceptualization, but rather invite comparison as "other ways" of dealing with *our own reality.* We incorporate them within our reality, and so incorporate their ways of life within our own self-invention. What we can perceive of the realities *they* have learned to invent and live in is relegated to the "supernatural" or dismissed as "merely symbolic."

Talking about nature in the context of culture, then, is a way of controlling culture. This is often a technique of advertisers, but is more familiarly a feature of the "ecology movement" in modern America. Discussing social abuses, the excesses of corporate industry, and other shortcomings of our collective Culture directly in social terms has the effect of calling our total conceptual system (our means of inventing our own "reality," that is) into question. A civilization that invents itself as man's relation to nature finds it more convenient and ideologically consistent (as well as much "safer") to deal with these inadequacies as abuses against "the environment," as "energy crisis," or "pollution." The ecology movement is thus an effort to control culture through nature, to criticize and curtail the massive and unthinking invention of natural force as "product" and "energy" in terms of the exhaustion and despoiling of its resource base. It is a "creative" inversion of the traditional "exploitive" point of view, a way of seeing culture as "something being done" to nature. Identifying with nature, the ecology activists are fundamentally concerned with the reform of Culture, with creating and restoring a balance between man's needs and their fulfillment—a balance, that is, within human society—*in the name of man's relation to nature.* Thus they are as much "conservative" as "conservationist," for in making the distinction between man's artificial "Culture" and an innate and circumambient "nature" the core of their "message," they reassert this distinction and the ideology based upon it.

Ecological approaches to anthropology can likewise be seen as attempts to control culture by talking about nature. Together with ancestral forms, such as the functionalism of Malinowski or the "culturology" of Leslie White, they are constituted in the form of "straight" science, objectifying culture by focusing on nature, natural "need," and the harnessing of energy. Ecological anthropology assumes that culture is an "adaptation" to a preexistent and universal natural reality. Different cultures, in this view, are different adaptations, often to different manifestations of nature (different "environments"). And although many ecological anthropologists are sensitive to the fact that cultures often play a large part in shaping their environments, the very nature of their inquiry keeps them from taking the next logical step—the conclusion that man creates his own realities. For they are committed as scientists to the study of nature, and to a view of reality that scientists must share with each other and with laymen if they are to communicate their findings. Just as nature serves as their control in the invention of individual cultures, so the unity of our conception of natural law and regularity serves them as a "common denominator" and standard of comparison for cultures. Without nature there would be no "science," no standard of evaluation, either in theoretical or in professional terms, for them.

In using our own reality as a control in the invention of cultures, inventing cultures that contrast with *part* of our conceptual scheme rather than the whole of it, ecological anthropology pays the price of ideological ethnocentrism. Whatever the natives "think" they are doing, their actions, ideas, and institutions are measured against the standard of our creativity, and the essence of their creativity is denatured and blurred over. We are unlikely to find an ecological anthropologist so naive as to deny that members of different cultures recognize and live in different "subjective" realities; the crucial point, however, involves the assessment of objective reality. If we insist on objectifying other cultures through *our* reality, we make *their* objectification of reality into a subjective illusion, a world of "mere symbols," other "classifications" of what "really is there." Hence the creativity of their invention of reality is subverted to our own, turning the thing that we apprehend as their culture into a strange and accidental metaphor of rationality, in Lévi-Strauss' term, a "science of the concrete."

Whenever we impose our conception and invention of reality on another culture, whether in the course of anthropology, missionizing, administration, or "development," we turn its indigenous creativity into something arbitrary and questionable, a mere symbolic word play. It becomes "another Culture," an analogue of our collective, rationally conceived enterprise of harnessing and interpreting natural reality, our opera-house Culture, which we also conceive of as arbitrary and symbolic in this sense. But since the whole force of human creativity lies in the ability to objectify, to identify symbolic elements *as* reality (to confuse them with reality, we might say) and "mask" their effects, what we "extend" to these subject cultures along with our conception of reality is our own "masking" of cultural creativity. Culture is recognized, indeed, but at the expense of its creativity. We have a commonplace habit of treating cultural orientations glibly as so many "myths," "interpretations of reality," or even "metaphors," as so many collective "mentalistic" illusions, while implicitly denying or ignoring their creative power and pervasiveness.

Most anthropologists are willing to include our Culture (our "myths," "interpretations of reality") in this category; that is what the traditional "culture-concept" and its much vaunted "relativity" are all about. But the acid test of any anthropology is whether it is willing to apply this relativity *objectively*—to our "reality" as well as to those of others—as well as *subjectively*. Unless we are able to do this, the creativity of the cultures we study will always be derivative of our own creation of reality. Unless we are able to *hold our own symbols responsible* for the reality we create with them, our notion of symbols and of culture in general will remain subject to the "masking" by which our invention conceals its effects. This *does not* mean that the anthropologist is obliged to "believe in" the realities of the peoples he studies, or that he is obliged to forego living and participating in his own culture. It implies rather that the individual who is able to penetrate the workings of invention and "belief" will be able to deal with meanings without being "used" by them. He will be a better anthropologist, a better citizen, and, for all of that, a better ecologist.

The notion of the "mere symbol," of meaning as an arbitrary construction, a perception "after the fact" of reality, is an artifact of our semantic commitment to natural reality. In this section we have reviewed the way in which this Culture of arbitrary symbols is objectified by a number of ("naturalistic") approaches through the use of "natural reality" as a control. This mode of inventing culture corresponds to the activity we normally think of as "science," the creative inversion of our ordinary objectification of nature that "recharges" its symbols and provides its means and facilities. But the other half of our conceptual world, the articulation of conventionalized contexts that we identify with "logic" and "rational thought," can also be used as a control on anthropological invention. Let us turn our attention now to the "logical" approaches that make this their aim.

Controlling nature

The controls of our collective Culture are generally understood as arbitrary and artificial, products of a cumulative historical ("Western" or "Judeo-Christian") development. To this extent they are felt to be learnable and teachable (this is what our "education" is all about), perfectible, and capable of amendation or change through innovation, legislation, or revolution. A rational state is an artificial one, with its origins grounded in some ideology of man's improvement and perfectibility. The signers of the American Declaration of Independence and the French revolutionaries who enthroned the goddess Reason believed themselves to be acting on the precedent of Rousseau's social contract. More modern rationalists trace their cultural ancestry in man's evolutionary development, the progress of science and technology, the evolution of jurisprudence and the state.

The guarantor of this enterprise, the ostensible reason for its existence and the standard against which its progress and self-perfection is measured, is an "innate" order of natural fact and natural law. The rational state is founded on the "natural rights" of its citizens, technology serves man's "natural needs," and science and natural philosophy strive to perfect their techniques, methodologies, and conceptual apparatus for the understanding and representation of "natural fact" and "reality." If we recognize this enterprise as a diverse and manifold invention of natural reality through all the means by which it is guarded, ensured, harnessed, and understood, then Cultural perfectibility is the guise in which this need for invention (and its motivation) appears. "Progress," "democracy," and "scientific certainty" are the masks worn by our collective invention of nature.

The activities, standards, procedures, techniques, and devices of our "official" and everyday Culture are all controls for the invention of the "innate" and "natural" part of our conceptual world. When we invoke them we not only mask the creative essence of our action behind the "realities" we create and the necessities they present to us, but we also reassert the ideological distinction between the "natural" and the "artificial." By inventing the "natural" as such we certify the distinction between "natural" and "Cultural," and the rationale that rests on this distinction. So the objectification of nature is as ineffective as the objectification of culture in the attempt to represent and understand an order that contrasts directly with our total conceptual scheme. When we use the collective and conventionalized controls of our Culture in this way, the effect is to re-create our own notions of the "natural" and "innate" in cultural form.

If naturalistic empiricism is basically an appeal to the effectiveness of our cultural controls in their invention of nature, that is, then the approaches that rely upon logical or "semantic" determinism appeal to our notion of the evolutionary or "cognitive" derivation of culture from an innate and preexistent natural order. They use complex and businesslike methodologies to investigate and determine (i.e., invent) *not* "culture"—in the sense of people dealing with each other and their surroundings—but nature (*our* nature) in its culturally "perceived" and "interpreted" form. They accept, virtually as an article of faith, the dogma that the arbitrary analogies, divisions, and distinctions that we have imposed upon the phenomenal world as "nature" are somehow innate and basic to it. They believe that plants, animals, colors, kinship, skin diseases are in some way "real" and self-evident *things,* rather than ways of talking about things.

This may seem a strange sort of faith for people who often like to identify themselves as linguists, but in fact it derives directly from our ideological assumptions about the nature of language. For language is a part of Culture, and is therefore seen as arbitrary, artificial, perfectible, and dependent upon definition and precise usage in the description of what is "real" and actual. Semantic anthropology relies on a common belief in the possibility and perfectibility of definitions —definitions grounded in collective assumptions about the innate and absolute existence of a single "real" phenomenal world—and it gives verbal denotation a deterministic priority over meaningful extension as a way of asserting the primacy of the "natural" order. It controls and produces "nature" through cultural means, insofar as a universal nature is the only phenomenal basis for the exactness of definitions, and the only phenomenal basis for eliciting "equivalent" definitions—translations—from its subjects.

Exact, denotative definitions of the kind that "ethnosemantic" anthropologists postulate and require are possible only to the extent that the "things" defined already exist as discrete entities. If we admit to the fact that language and meaning create reality, instead of vice versa, then the priority of denotation (the evolutionary or "cognitive" derivation of cultural category from natural order) is called into question. The kind of "translation" upon which ethnosemantic procedures depend is possible only insofar as the same overall "reality" of discrete "things" is shared by speakers of the two languages concerned, for how else can denotative definitions be "translated" from one to the other? Once it is agreed that this postulated universal reality exists, then the peculiar tendencies and conformations of the informants' responses (the outline of their "categories") can be explained away as different *classifications* of the world of real things.

The whole effort of semantic anthropology emerges as an exercise in verifying (and thus creating) the existence of the universal reality it postulates. It objectifies "nature" through the conscious manipulation of culture, inventing a single, universal "reality" through the translative "elicitation" of "cognitive categories." Its techniques of eliciting responses and determining "domains" and "paradigms" are in fact devices for collapsing meaningful utterances into the denotative definitions that are assumed to have cognitive priority, for forcing the flow of invention into the straitjacket of definition. They are methodologies for transforming other peoples' responses into the objectification ("cognition," "categorization," "classification") of natural reality, which is therefore invented through the manipulation of other peoples' "cultural" controls rather than through our own. It is this interest in the priority of natural order, leading to an "epistemology" of nature recognizing itself through "cognition," that provides the excuse and the stimulus for "ethnography," for the exploration of cognition on a worldwide scale.

Of course semantic anthropologists do not see themselves as inventing or objectifying nature, for their methodological controls are grounded in the assumption of natural innateness. Their self-confirmation of the postulated reality is masked as a quest for "scientific certainty," a need to improve the articulation of the controls, devise methodologies, sharpen up definitions, and retrieve more data. Any attempt at criticism of their approach is referred directly to the interests of this collective effort and not to its underlying assumptions.

They feel that criticism should be phrased in such a way as to help create better methodologies, improve definitions, and operationalize the retrieval of data. The suggestion that these methodologies confirm their data by presupposing the reality on which it is based would be regarded as subversive to the honest efforts of dedicated professionals. Let us sum up our observations in the form of a methodological suggestion: The most efficacious methodology for semantic anthropology is one that analyzes the way man creates his own realities, beginning with the procedures of "ethnosemantics" itself.

I have argued that man creates his realities through objectification, giving his thoughts, acts, and products the characteristics of certain contexts selected as "controls." Semantic anthropology is interesting because it uses objectification to deny the existence of objectification. By a kind of "artificial conventionalization" it reduces meaningful expression to language, to a set of elicited definitions, which in turn serve as a means of objectifying the natural world. The efforts and techniques of ethnosemantics, and, as a last resort, the "categories" of the natives themselves, provide the masking for this objectification. Thus the control of nature through culture reasserts the primacy and innateness of the natural and the "artificiality" and "arbitrariness" of the cultural, and reinforces the ideology that corresponds to it.

The approaches known generally as "ethnoscience" or "ethnosemantics" represent highly specialized and elaborated versions of a much older and more widespread tendency in anthropology. The "translation" of other peoples' verbal expressions, usages, and customs into a set of conscious "rules," "laws," "grammars"—into analogues of our Culture—amounts to a use of cultural controls, and hence a "borrowing" of the forms of other cultures (whatever their original significance) for application in our invention of nature. This does much to explain why even the most eclectic and traditionalist anthropologists maintain an implicit faith in the "natural" and evolutionary basis of man's culture, and in the innateness of "natural" phenomena. It is the thing they invent, and the thing their anthropology has taught them to invent.

Perhaps the best example of this almost universal anthropological invention and control of natural reality comes from the study of "kinship." In his comprehensive overview of kinship studies since the beginnings of anthropological inquiry, "What Is Kinship All About?" Schneider demonstrates that the putative existence and continued recognition of a discrete domain of "kinship" is predicated upon a belief in the innate and self-evident nature of, and the priority of, biological and genealogical "fact." It is the very "facticity" of this "natural fact" that permits the definition of the domain, delimiting its boundaries and demarcating its components along allegedly "natural" or "factual" lines. In Schneider's words:

> The two sides of "kinship," the biological model (whether real or presumptive, putative or fictive) and the social relationship (the rights, duties, privileges, roles, and statuses) stand in a hierarchical relationship to each other, for the biological defines the system to which the social is attached, and is thus logically prior to the latter.[2]

He shows that this hierarchical relationship, with its commitment to the priority of natural fact, has been accepted by virtually *all* theories and theorists of kin relations since the days of Louis Henry Morgan—by Rivers and Radcliffe-Brown, by Kroeber and the componential analysts, as well as by such innovative thinkers as Leach and Lévi-Strauss.

Why this incredible tenacity, we might ask, why this century or more of maneuvering, reconnoitering, and trimming one's sails within the confines of a single "paradigm"? There can be only one answer, and one motive: the necessity of a culture, or its members, to substantiate and confirm, to invent, a particular reality. In order to do this, it is necessary to believe in one's ability to do it. The "fact'" of "natural kinship" makes the definition of "kinship" possible. By subscribing to "kinship" as a research concept, a means of operation, a control, by proceeding *as if it were* a definable paradigm with a limited and derivable set of discrete terms, by eliciting the defining terms and hence creating the definitions, we objectify the thing defined. The strongest impulse in traditional kinship studies has been the substantiation and re-creation of our culture's "reality." This has made kinship studies (as well as the "social anthropology" to which they belong) a part of our cultural self-invention rather than a critique of that invention or a general inquiry into man's self-invention.

The anthropology of controlling nature is just as close to—and just as far from—the conclusion that man invents his own realities as the anthropology of controlling culture. Here, too, it is our "Culture," with its unquestioned and unanalyzed assumptions about what is "real" and how to go about studying it, that gets in the way. The theories and professional identity of an ecological anthropologist stem from a faith in the primacy and innateness of the "natural," masking a commitment to the ultimate effectiveness of the scientific and "Cultural" controls through which we describe and analyze (invent) nature.

2. David M. Schneider, "What Is Kinship All About," in *Kinship Studies in the Morgan Centennial Year*, ed. P. Reining (Washington, D.C.: Washington Anthropological Society, 1972).

The theories and professional identity of the traditional "cultural" anthropologist stem from a faith in the importance of culture that masks an implicit faith in the innateness of a natural reality as the guarantor of culture. It is but a step from the findings of many sensitive and intelligent ecologists that man helps to shape his environment, or from the awareness of many equally sophisticated cultural anthropologists that man "interprets" or "understands" his surroundings through his own categories, to the conclusion that man creates his realities. But for people with unquestioned and unanalyzed commitments of the sort I have been discussing, it is a giant step indeed. And yet I would argue that it is a necessary and inevitable one.

The writings of Claude Lévi-Strauss and his followers and antagonists among the "Structuralists," of Louis Dumont, Edmund Leach, and other innovators of modern cultural anthropology have played an indispensable role in preparing anthropology for the kind of self-awareness that a theory based on invention implies. Yet these writers, too, have generally fought shy of completely relativistic conclusions—largely, we might suspect, in the interests of preserving and "protecting" the cultural and scientific perspectives that allow their theories to be communicated. I leave it to the reader to determine the extent to which this strategy of "protecting anthropology from itself" is advisable. Lévi-Strauss, for instance, embarked upon his brilliant and fascinating study of South American mythology in the conviction that:

> Mythology has no obvious practical function: unlike the phenomena previously studied, it is not directly linked with a different kind of reality, which is endowed with a higher degree of objectivity than its own and whose injunctions it might therefore transmit to minds that seem perfectly free to indulge their creative spontaneity.[3]

Yet this intellectual expedition to track the imagination to its lair sets out with some very Western presuppositions about the nature of "myth" in relation to "reality" and about the universality of natural phenomena. It begins by stating that:

> The aim of this book is to show how empirical categories—such as the categories of the raw and the cooked, the fresh and the decayed, the moistened and the burned, etc., which can only be accurately defined by ethnographic observation and, in each instance, by adopting the standpoint of a particular culture—can nonetheless be used as conceptual tools with which to elaborate abstract ideas and combine them in the form of propositions.[4]

3. Claude Lévi-Strauss, *The Raw and the Cooked: Introduction to a Science of Mythology: I*, tr. *John and Doreen Weightman* (New York and Evanston, Ill.: Harper & Row, 1969), p. 10.
   4. Ibid., p. 1.

If the reader will flip back a few pages to my discussion of semantic anthropology, he will find that these aims correspond exactly with my characterization of ethnosemantics as the objectification of nature through native category. I will, therefore, have to beg Professor Lévi-Strauss's forgiveness (and, I am afraid, that of the ethnosemanticists as well) and classify him as an ethnosemanticist. To borrow a metaphor from Robert Frost, we might say that he plays ethnosemantic tennis "with the net down," that is, without benefit of elicitational method-ologies. (Though it would only be fair to recall Carl Sandberg's re-joinder to Frost's criticism of free verse: one can play better tennis with the net down.)

I do not mean to create the impression that all anthropologists are trapped within the objectification of nature through culture, or vice versa. Pioneers like Lévi-Strauss, Dumont, and Leach deserve every credit for forging the conceptual apparatus that has brought a self-analytic anthropology within the range of possibility. Many younger anthropologists have followed the lead of David M. Schneider and Clifford Geertz in carrying their inquiries and conclusions beyond the bounds set for them by a traditionalistic anthropology and by staid academicism. Anthropological studies that objectify cultures as self-creative analogues of our total conceptual system, rather than our rationalistic Culture in its narrow sense, that are not caught up in the trap of using one set of our cultural controls to implicitly invent the other, stand in an innovative and evaluative relationship to our con-ceptual system as a whole. They are not a part of our invention of reality, of our derivation of Culture from nature or vice versa, and their conclusions are therefore not necessarily subject to the "masking" that imprisons its operations within a kind of subliminal ethnocen-trism. An anthropology that invents culture rather than "our Culture" through the unqualified and universal application of concepts like the dialectic, objectification, and mediation implies self-analysis as a necessary part of the analysis of others, and vice versa.

The end of synthetic anthropology

What is this traditional "science of man," with its reifications of tradition and custom, its evolution, its "superorganic," and its syn-thetic world view of "cultural" phenomena balanced precariously on an academic house of cards labeled "chemistry," "biology," "psychol-ogy," "political science?" In every way it is a worthy and analogous contemporary of advertising, a culture-cult precipatating its ultimate rationale through the zealous pursuit of particular "brands" of theory. It is a way of having cultural relativity and eating it too, a fast and loose "playing" with invention and experience in such a way that our commitment to Culture and collective enterprise is always vindicated.

Relativity has always been vital to anthropology, which underwent many of its formative crises and transformations contemporaneously with the development of relativity in physics. The era that has included the self-searching of physicists from Mach and Einstein to Heisenberg and the examination of anthropological concept from Tylor through Boas, Kroeber, and Goldenweiser to Lévi-Strauss and Schneider is a phase in the growing self-consciousness of a progressively relativizing and self-obviating Culture. Its advances are precious beyond computation, and destructive in the extreme. They threaten the very fabric of our academic and secular social order, *but they also sustain this order by giving it a challenge and a relevance, something to talk about.* They revivify it, as the absurd nuisance of advertising revivifies our economic life. Serious introspection in anthropology leads inevitably to the unmasking of its theories and problems. And yet, when administered in small doses, this kind of insight provides the motivation and stimulus that keeps the science alive.

Every advance into the perilous realm of relative insight precipitates a scholarly "literature" and "knowledge" as its antithesis. Each grain of introspection is "applied" and developed by busy scientific industries. Our massed libraries of ethnography and theory are in this respect learned reverberations of vital critical earthquakes. Indeed, the temptation is great to speak of a sequence of "paradigms" in the sense of Thomas Kuhn's theory of scientific revolutions,[5] except for the fact that the "paradigms" are crucially locked into ever larger matrices of development and change, which might also be seen as paradigms. The whole of anthropology, in its hundred-year academic career, falls into sequence with broader developments, with Hobbes' conception of society as "a mortall God," with Rousseau, Kant, Hegel, and the theories of human evolution and degeneration. And there is as much play between the "disciplines," and across the academic keyboards on which paradigms are performed, as within them. Kuhn's theory makes more sense as an overall appreciation of change than as phenomenal description. It ought to be rewritten from the standpoint of invention.

Consider the broadest outlines of anthropological history. The "diachronic" or "historical" anthropology of Tylor, Morgan, and the German, British, and American diffusionists led to a kind of theoretical exhaustion that made "synchronic" and systemic concerns urgent

5. Thomas S. Kuhn, *The Structure of Scientific Revolutions* (Chicago: University of Chicago Press, 1964).

and important. This later epoch, that of Malinowskian and Radcliffe-Brownian "functionalism" and Lévi-Straussian "structuralism" and cognitive anthropology gave rise, in turn, to a very real modern theoretical bankruptcy. Both "kinds" of anthropology, that which treated "cultures" as parts of a geographical-historical "system," and that which treated of individual "cultures" as systems in their own right, can be considered as a single paradigm or as separate paradigms. Each can also be resolved into constituent paradigms. The evolutionism of Tylor and Morgan, among others, obviated itself in the years between 1870 and 1895, and set the stage for Frobenius' formulation of historicogeographical diffusionism in the 1890s, and for Graebner's foundation of the *Kulturkreislehre* in 1904. But by the time of the First World War Graebner had identified his "Melanesian Bow Culture" on all five continents, Frobenius had already abandoned his earlier creation, and Malinowski was beginning his fieldwork. What followed was a sweeping critical insight that took the historical issues for granted and made systemic ones problematic, just as the earlier anthropology had reversed this order. Functionalism saw "cultures" as social mechanisms, configurationalism (Frobenius, Spengler, Kroeber, Sapir, Benedict, and later Redfield) saw them as sociopsychological "patterns": both emphasized their integration. But culture as integrated system was vulnerable to criticism of ethnocentricity—in order to demonstrate systemic "functioning" or "patterning" it took the conceptualization of cultural things for granted. And so, beginning with Lévi-Strauss' *Elementary Structures of Kinship* (1949), and continuing through his later writings and those of the ethnoscientists, culture was explained as a logical and consistent (rather than a functional and efficient) system. Whereas functionalism and configurationalism took the conceptual order of things for granted and made integration problematic, structuralism and ethnoscience took integration for granted (in the form of "reciprocity") and made conceptualization problematic.

None of these epochs and transformations was independent of other events. Historical anthropology mirrored the ideology of the late colonial and supraethnic empires of Britain, France, Central Europe, and others. (These empires quite literally "did" Cultural evolution and diffusion as a matter of policy.) Systemic anthropology reflected the rational urgency of wartime mobilization and the economic nation-state. The curious "evolution" in which each of the successive paradigmatic episodes worked itself into an obviation and contradiction of its original assumptions provides the most compelling evidence for the nature of anthropology as an academic discipline. It is a holding action against relativity, a kind of theoretical fixative that builds introspective insight into culturally supportive theory. Progressively sharper and more compelling critical insights were born of the failure of each successive holding action, and in every instance these insights were used as the groundwork for new synthetic theories. It is a science that lives by continually *postponing* the implications of its ideas, implications whose postponement leads ultimately to critical and introspective leaps.

What is the whole corpus of British social anthropology, of "descent theory" and the "corporate group," but an attempt to explain tribal society as a juro-economic "Establishment," to precipitate Culture *as Establishment* at the expense of critical relativity? Nor is British social anthropology uniquely culpable in this respect. We have an ecological functionalism that sacrifices the relativity of invention to the reality of natural law, an ethnoscience that buys its theoretical and professional certainty at the expense of acknowledging its subjects' creativity. Even the much-touted synthesis that anthropologists of the late 1960s and early 1970s made of the insights of Mauss, Lévi-Strauss, and the (other) logical determinists, the "Cartesian" duality of reciprocity and classification, is a resolution of invention into two artificial poles that threaten to collapse into one another at any moment. Indeed, they must collapse to be factual at all!

At most, reciprocity is the understanding that things assumed to be "equal" in value (whether objects, rights, obligations, tokens, or other "cultural" elements) are exchanged. But what makes exchange interesting, worthwhile, fun, profitable, and workable is the fact that the things being exchanged are unequal from the standpoints of the respective exchangers. So reciprocity amounts to an assumption of the equality of things in the context of their being unequal, to facilitate a resulting inequality of exchangers in the context of their ostensible equality as parties to the exchange. Taken as a whole, reciprocity has the metaphoric quality of handling equality and inequality simultaneously—it can be what you make it depending on how you choose to interpret it. Thus not only is reciprocity reducible to the proposition that people tend to place relative valuations on things, but this proposition is further reducible to the fact that these values are created and changed constantly in the act of referring to or dealing with them.

Classification, on the other hand, is an understanding that one kind of thing will stand for another, or particularize or exemplify some class to which it is assigned, which is the same thing. But the act of classification can only be understood as meaningful or provocative if the one thing is in some way understood *not* to stand for or exemplify the class of the other. The alternative, assigning a thing to stand for something that it already is, or using it to exemplify itself as a class, is tautology. The act becomes meaningful by cross-cutting categories; as the Russians are fond of saying, *izvestia nye pravda i pravda nye izvestia,* "the news isn't the truth and the truth isn't news." Classification becomes meaningful and provocative, becomes an act or event, becomes "news," when and if it impinges upon the "truth" of accepted values and categories. But then, one could argue, it is no longer classification but reclassification, and the difference is a crucial one. So the static world of categories can only be activated and realized through acts of reevaluation that turn its classes into events, just as the actional world of reciprocity can only be deciphered by reducing its acts to the creation of values. The alternative is a universe of actionless meanings and meaningless actions.

If each pole can be collapsed into the other, then the polarity itself is meaningless. And so is the anthropology that addresses itself to the phenomenal reality of reciprocity by collapsing an implicit world of values into an explicit interplay of exchanges, or that which reifies an ordered world of logical categories by subsuming and collapsing an implicit world of motion and event. That which is subsumed or collapsed is referred to as another "level," and the universe of phenomenal levels (of particular "subject matters," each of which is defined by operations of this kind) is a fragile hierarchy of reductions, which ultimately resolves into the polarity of the innate versus the artificial. "Fact" emerges as the mask of a whole realm of theoretical contradictions; each operation encompasses the dialectical and contradictory aspect of the interrelation of "levels" in its setting up, and then abolishes and collapses it in the derivation of "fact." So the "orders" or "levels" represent a series of repetitive and tautological "reductions" of a single inventive potentiality via the objectifications of our various theoretical techniques ("methodologies" and so forth) of fact production. The synthetic world of science is a world of patched-together consistency.

It does not matter whether we apprehend the various "approaches" of anthropology (or the broader spectrum comprising those of science itself) as a developmental sequence of successive "contributions" to a comprehensive arsenal of theory, or conceive them "synchronically" as attempts to deal with the various "levels" of reality. It does not matter, in other words, whether we choose to rationalize the dialectic in historical terms as a parade of human achievement, or in "natural" terms as an order of phenomenal levels. It all comes down to the same thing: an intellectual banishment of invention and the relativity of convention in the interests of supporting *our own* conventional world— the metamorphosis of man's creation of reality into our conventional orders of "knowledge" and "fact."

The era that anthropology is now outgrowing is that of synthesism, in its diachronic or historical-diffusionist manifestation (1871–1922) and its synchronic-systemic one (1922–1972). The basis of synthetic anthropology was the idea that "levels" of phenomena correspond to the branches of academic study (physical, biological, and social sciences). Its great triumphs were the "superorganic" of Kroeber, the "levels" of White and Steward, and the grand syntheses of Talcott Parsons. When it overshot itself, as it did many times in the writings of Benedict, Bateson, Sapir, Lévi-Strauss, and later of Schneider and his students, it drew heavy fire from those who wondered whether the other "levels," the economic and natural "facts," were being slighted.

And so anthropology and its motto-concept "culture" is not so much an inquiry into the phenomenal world as a stage in our own Cultural relativization and the wakening understanding that it both brings and requires. Culture is what you make it, though it poses the same kind of trap for those who would consider it as "real" as any other concept. As a messianic device, a road to "freedom" for those who would seek enthusiasm through which to bring their Culture to life again, its future potentialities are *extensive* rather than *intensive*. It will expand and proliferate mightily as a wave-front of incipient sophistication, drawing students and laymen alike into the exciting game of building and reaffirming Culture out of its own perilous contradiction in the form of exotic experience. The step beyond it is the point at which the play and the contradiction become more important than the affirmation of Culture.

This contradiction is essentially the way in which anthropology has invented itself in the developmental outline I have presented, though this perspective is and must be denied by the mask that anthropology wears as a synthetic discipline. Anthropology as a part of Culture is an accumulation of great ideas, insights, and works, and its professional image presents this "literature" as a set of more or less equally viable theoretical possibilities. It is possible to buy textbooks that set forth these "contributions" in just this way, minimizing and underplaying their contradictions, and obliterating their dialectical continuity. "Go mine the literature" say the elder statesmen, and the publishers of ever more comprehensive "readers," "and you'll find what you're looking for—it's all been said before." And, of course, it very nearly has been. What this academic amnesia, this white-out of invention via the printed page amounts to is merely a more staid and institutionalized theater in the battle against cultural relativization and the consciousness of cultural relativity that it brings. Textbook anthropology is a catalogue of the devices that theory has used to check and overcome relativity; it brings the synthetic world of midcentury science, with its levels and reductionisms, all together again. Definitions restore the "clarity" and security of commonplace secular reality; great men and their mystical, anecdotal auras restore confidence in the slogging progressiveness of "tradition," and the science that stands in need of this kind of ideological furniture can always find likely candidates, or make them up.

If this discussion has seemed a bit overly critical of assumptions that have heretofore been sacrosanct, if it has continually addressed the question of what science *does not want to know,* rather than what it does want to know, then perhaps we ought to examine the need for such criticism more closely. For the perspective I have developed here is not simply anomalous or divergent from our academic and secular ideologies, but directly contradictory of them. It suggests that the very realities upon which we base our theories, actions, and institutions are contrivances of human invention and conventional interpretation. It implies that academia has been the handmaiden of the other interests committed to the invention of our secular reality.

Assumptions of this sort have heretofore been shunned by anthropologists fearful of compromising their basis of inquiry, the groundwork of consistency upon which the rationalism of science is founded. The preeminence of Culture, in short, has never been seriously challenged. But the progressive relativization that has come about through the very conservatism that this stance exemplifies has obviated our Culture and its solutions and institutions to the point where the study of culture is directly involved in a critique that transcends the purely academic. It is not that the times have become worse, or that the people have become more honest—or even, alas, that the "truth" is slowly coming out (as it always has been). It is that a progressively relativizing Culture progressively obviates its own interests and activities, and its operations become increasingly obvious in the process.

In this situation anthropology can no more afford to play Grand Inquisitor, concealing the workings of invention from people "for their own good," than commercial or administrative interests can. Destructive as this may be to a certain conservative and conservatively defended social order, the whole anatomy of invention, the implications surrounding it, and the responsibility it entails must be articulated openly and publicly. This is a social and political *duty,* and our only alternative to being victimized by the inventors and manipulators of secular reality. We can learn to use invention, or else be used by it. If undertaken responsibly and carefully, this learning can lead to a harmonious regime of trust and understanding between the creatively opposed segments of society. And the task of building an awareness of invention constitutes the goal and culmination of the social sciences.

The future of Western society lies in its ability to create social forms that will make explicit distinctions between classes and segments of society, *so that these distinctions do not come of themselves as implicit racism, discrimination, corruption, crises, riots, necessary "cheating" and "finagling," and so on.* The future of anthropology lies in its ability to exorcise "difference" and make it conscious and explicit, both with regard to its subject matter and to itself. Especially in America,[6] we have an "anthropology of fact and faction," focusing explicitly on factual consistency, knowledge, and professional brotherhood, but full of implicit and furtive differences, rivalries, jealousies, and quite unprofessional ambitions that are the more destructive (and politically vicious) for being unspoken. It is a fact-producing "industry" that *suffers* the dialectic as history, polemic, and factional squabble, living a cultic succession of jargons, bandwagons, and "needs" of the department or the discipline, "setting up" its own surreptitious revolutions and cataclysms by projecting optimistic and unrealistic "programs" for concerted action.

Our much celebrated "Western history" is in fact invention placed "out of awareness"; it is dialectic experienced as event, as nature. Whether we call this dialectic a "class struggle" (which it often is), "the rise and decline of high cultural organisms" (which it clevely mimics), "man's struggle with nature within him and around him" (its operating illusion), or "evolution" (dialectic as nature, "natural history"), the one necessity that it presents to us is that we bring it into awareness. And so, too, the only alternative to an anthropology that obviates its own theories as its "history" is an anthropology founded on the deliberate and conscious recognition of dialectic and the implications of obviation.

What does all of this mean in terms of anthropology's professional future? Obviously it entails some major revisions in theory as well as in the way in which we conceive of the discipline itself. Above all, anthropology should proceed, like good fieldwork, in full awareness of difference and contradiction. The inherent contradictions in the vari-

---

6. I am grateful to Laura Bohannan and Pedro Armillas for pointing out that the more stable scholarly and professional bodies of England and Germany make the deliberate statement of theoretical differences a matter of traditional procedure.

ous theoretical approaches should be made explicit and be used to elicit an implicit professional community. The ethics and methodologies of fieldwork should become "transparent" to the creativity being studied. We should subordinate their assumptions and preconceptions to the inventiveness of the "subject peoples," *so as not to preempt their creativity within our own invention.* And the presentation of the anthropological "literature" as "fact," "data," or "knowledge" must be tempered by the kind of interpretation (like the "hermaneutics" advocated by Johannes Fabian, Jürgen Habermas, and others) that will bring the fascinating and mutual invention of anthropologist and "native" alike into awareness.

Voltaire observed that if God did not exist it would have been necessary to invent Him. And, like the theologians of the Islamic Muta'zilla, I would add that if God *does* exist, this makes it all the more necessary that we invent Him, for invention is the form of our experience and understanding. If we have anything to learn from these "enlightened" thinkers and philosophies of the past (which were as much "illusory" as anything else), it is that man should not quibble about the existence or nonexistence of such illusions, but rather exercise his categorical right to choose among them. And so the reader should feel free to indulge his own faith in the ultimate existence of God, or nature, or natural law, over and above our invention of them, and over and above anything we may discover about this invention. It is, after all, a very human thing to do. In Nietzsche's phrasing, "all too human."

Index